PRENTICE HALL

Student Handbook

FORENSIC SCIENCE

PEARSON

Boston, Massachusetts
Chandler, Arizona
Glenview, Illinois
Upper Saddle River, New Jersey

PRENTICE HALL
Forensic Science

Resources

- Student Edition
- Teacher's Guide
- Student Handbook
- Student Handbook, Annotated Teacher's Edition
- Chapter and Unit Tests
- Forensic Science Videos
- Materials Kits

13-digit ISBN 978-0-13-362748-0
10-digit ISBN 0-13-362748-9

3 4 5 6 7 8 9 10   12 11 10 09

Contents

Laboratory Safety

To keep yourself and your classmates safe during lab activities, you need to do three things. (1) Become familiar with the general rules for working in a lab. Those rules are summarized below. (2) Before you start an activity, be sure to read the Safety First! section. Also listen carefully to your teacher's instructions. If you are not sure how to do a step in the procedure, don't be afraid to ask questions. (3) Do not fool around during a lab activity. Such behavior can result in an injury to you or a classmate.

General Precautions

Never perform lab activities without the approval and supervision of your teacher. Do not engage in horseplay during activities. Never eat or drink in the area where you are doing lab activities. Keep work areas clean and uncluttered.

Protective Clothing

Wear safety goggles whenever you work with chemicals, glassware, heat sources such as burners, or any substance that might get into your eyes. If you wear contact lenses, notify your teacher.

Wear a lab apron and disposable plastic gloves whenever you work with corrosive chemicals or substances that can stain. Tie back long hair. Remove or tie back any article of clothing or jewelry that can hang down and touch chemicals, flames, or equipment. Roll up long sleeves. Do not wear open shoes or sandals.

First Aid

Report all accidents, injuries, or fires to your teacher, no matter how minor. Be aware of the location of the first-aid kit, emergency equipment such as the fire extinguisher and fire blanket, and the nearest telephone. Know whom to contact in an emergency.

Using Chemicals Safely

Never put your face near the mouth of a container that holds chemicals. Never touch, taste, or smell a chemical unless your teacher tells you to.

Use only those chemicals needed in an activity. Keep all containers closed when chemicals are not being used. Pour all chemicals over the sink or a container, not over your work surface. Dispose of extra chemicals as instructed by your teacher.

Be extra careful when working with acids or bases. When mixing an acid and water, always pour the water into the container first and then add the acid to the water. Never pour water into an acid. Wash chemical spills and splashes immediately with plenty of water.

Heating and Fire Safety

Keep all flammable materials away from flames. When heating a substance in a test tube, make sure the mouth of the tube is not pointed at you or anyone else. Never heat a liquid in a closed container. Use an oven mitt to pick up a container that has been heated.

Using Glassware Safely

If glassware is broken or chipped, notify your teacher immediately. Never handle broken or chipped glass with your bare hands.

Never force glass tubing or thermometers into a rubber stopper or rubber tubing. Have your teacher insert the glass tubing or thermometer if required for an activity.

Using Sharp Instruments

Handle sharp instruments with extreme care. Never cut material toward you; cut away from you.

Animal and Plant Safety

Never perform experiments that cause pain, discomfort, or harm to animals. Only handle animals if absolutely necessary. If you know that you are allergic to certain plants, molds, or animals, tell your teacher before doing an activity in which these are used. Wash your hands thoroughly with soap and warm water after any activity that involves touching animals, animal parts, plants, plant parts, or soil.

During field work, wear long pants, long sleeves, socks, and closed shoes. Avoid poisonous plants and fungi as well as plants with thorns.

End-of-Experiment Rules

Unplug all electrical equipment. Clean up your work area. Dispose of waste materials as instructed by your teacher. Wash your hands with soap and warm water after every experiment.

Safety Symbols

These symbols warn of possible dangers in the laboratory activities and remind you to work carefully.

Safety Goggles Wear safety goggles to protect your eyes in any activity involving chemicals, flames or heating, or glassware.

Lab Apron Wear a laboratory apron to protect your skin and clothing from damage.

Plastic Gloves Wear disposable plastic gloves when working with harmful chemicals and organisms. Keep your hands away from your face, and dispose of the gloves according to your teacher's instructions.

Heat-Resistant Gloves Use an oven mitt or other hand protection when handling hot materials such as hot plates or hot glassware.

Breakage Handle breakable materials, such as glassware, with care. Do not touch broken glassware.

Heating Use a clamp or tongs to pick up hot glassware. Do not touch hot objects with your bare hands.

Flames Before you work with flames, tie back loose hair and clothing. Follow instructions from your teacher about lighting and extinguishing flames.

No Flames When using flammable materials, make sure there are no flames, sparks, or other exposed heat sources present.

Corrosive Chemical Avoid getting acid or other corrosive chemicals on your skin or clothing or in your eyes. Do not inhale the vapors. Wash your hands with soap and warm water after the activity.

Poison Do not let any poisonous chemical come into contact with your skin, and do not inhale its vapors. Wash your hands with soap and warm water when you are finished with the activity.

Fumes Work in a ventilated area when harmful vapors may be involved. Avoid inhaling vapors directly. Only test an odor when directed to do so by your teacher, and use a wafting motion to direct the vapor toward your nose.

Sharp Object Scissors, scalpels, knives, needles, pins, and tacks can cut your skin. Always direct a sharp edge or point away from yourself and others.

Animal Safety Treat live or preserved animals or animal parts with care to avoid harming the animals or yourself. Wash your hands with soap and warm water when you are finished with the activity.

Plant Safety Handle plants only as directed by your teacher. If you are allergic to certain plants, tell your teacher. Do not do an activity involving those plants. Avoid touching harmful plants such as poison ivy. Wash your hands with soap and warm water when you are finished with the activity.

Electric Shock To avoid electric shock, never use electrical equipment around water, or when the equipment is wet or your hands are wet. Be sure cords are untangled and cannot trip anyone. Unplug equipment not in use.

Physical Safety When an experiment involves physical activity, avoid injuring yourself or others. Alert your teacher if there is any reason you should not participate.

Disposal Dispose of chemicals and other laboratory materials safely. Follow the instructions from your teacher.

Hand Washing Wash your hands thoroughly with soap and warm water when you are finished with the activity. Rinse well.

General Safety Awareness When this symbol appears, follow the instructions provided. When you are asked to develop your own procedure in a lab, have your teacher approve your plan before you go further.

Chapter 1   Building Science Vocabulary

High-Use Academic Words

High-use academic words are words that are used frequently in class-rooms. You and your teachers use these words when you discuss topics in science and other subjects. Look for the words in the table below as you read this chapter.

Word	Definition	Sample Sentence
interpret (in TUR prut) pp. 6, 10	v. to find or explain the meaning of	The English teacher asked her students to <u>interpret</u> a poem.
identify (eye DEN tuh fy) pp. 13, 23, 25, 26, 28, 35	v. to recognize as being a specific person or thing	Some birds can <u>identify</u> their chicks by the sounds the chicks make.
process (PRAH ses) p. 10	n. a series of actions or events; a particular way of doing things	During the rehearsal <u>process</u>, the actors learned where to enter and exit the stage.
transfer (TRANS fur) pp. 30, 34, 35	v. to move a person or thing from one place to another	When you touch wet paint, you <u>transfer</u> paint to your hands.
pattern (PAT urn) p. 33	n. an orderly arrangement of parts; a model or plan used as a guide	The <u>pattern</u> the marching band made looked like the letter *W*.

Apply It!

Choose the word that best completes each sentence.

1. The witness could not _____ the thief.

2. The wallpaper has a repeating _____ of flowers and leaves.

3. One step in the bread-making _____ is letting the dough rise.

4. The detective could not _____ the note left at the crime scene.

Building Science Vocabulary (continued)

Identify Related Word Forms

You can increase your vocabulary by learning related forms of a word. For example, if you know that the noun *influence* means "the power to affect others," you can figure out that the adjective *influential* can describe a person who has the power to affect others. The table below shows some related word forms for terms from Chapter 1.

Key Term	Meaning	Related Word Forms
predicting *v.*	stating an opinion about what will happen in the future	**prediction** *n.* the event that is predicted **predictable** *adj.* able to be predicted
crime scene investigator *n.*	a person who is trained to record, collect, and test evidence from a crime scene	**investigate** *v.* to search into so as to learn the facts **investigation** *n.* a careful search or examination
chain of custody *n.*	a written record of who had control of evidence from the time it was collected	**custodian** *n.* a person responsible for the care of an object
evidence *n.*	something that can be used to prove a fact	**evident** *adj.* easy to see; clear or obvious

Apply It!

Review the words related to predicting. *Complete the following sentences with the correct form of the word.*

1. Hurricane Angelo damaged orange groves in Central Florida.

   Experts are _____ that the price of oranges will rise.

2. After the heavy rain, some flooding was _____.

Lesson 1-1 · Reading and Note Taking Guide

Using Science to Solve Crimes (pages 6–13)

Science at a Crime Scene (pages 7–9)

Key Concept: The investigative team uses inquiry skills to help solve crimes. These skills include observing, inferring, predicting, and developing a hypothesis.

▶ **Forensic science** is the use of scientific knowledge and methods to solve crimes and answer legal questions.

▶ **Observing** is the use of one or more senses to gather information.

▶ Investigators look for evidence at a crime scene. **Evidence** is something that can be presented in court to make a point during a trial. Evidence can be an item collected at a crime scene or the results of tests done on that item.

▶ **Inferring** is offering a reasoned opinion based on observations and experience. **Predicting** is stating an opinion about what will happen in the future.

▶ A **hypothesis** is a possible explanation for a set of observations.

Use your textbook and the ideas above to answer these questions.

1. Choose a word from the box to complete each sentence below.

inferring	predicting	observing

   a. When you use your senses, you are _____.

   b. When you offer an opinion about something that may happen in the future, you are _____.

2. Is the following statement true or false? Every clue found at a crime scene is useful as evidence in court. _____

3. What do investigators use to support or reject a hypothesis?

   _____

   _____

Teamwork at a Crime Scene (pages 10–11)

Key Concept: Each member of an investigative team brings specific skills and knowledge to the team. Each has an assigned role.

▶ Uniformed police officers almost always respond first to a 9-1-1 call. Fire and ambulance crews may also be sent to a crime scene.

▶ A **crime scene investigator (CSI)** is trained to record, collect, and test evidence from a crime scene.

▶ When there is a sudden or suspicious death, a **medical examiner** will come to observe the body. The doctor may later do a detailed exam of the body called an **autopsy** (AW tahp see).

Use your textbook and the ideas above to answer these questions.

4. Is the following statement true or false? The first responsibility of the team at a crime scene is to save lives. _____

5. Each member of a crime scene team has a specific job. Draw a line from each team member in Column 1 to a task he or she does in Column 2.

Team Member	Role
medical examiner	**a.** uses bones to figure out how a victim died
crime scene investigator	**b.** treats victims at a crime scene
forensic anthropologist	**c.** estimates a victim's time of death
emergency medical technician	**d.** collects and tests crime scene evidence

Forensic Science Methods (pages 12–13)

Key Concept: Scientists still design tests to solve crimes. But now they have better technology for doing the tests.

▶ The Greek scientist Archimedes used a property of matter called density to solve a crime. **Density** is the ratio of the mass of a substance to its volume.

▶ Modern forensic scientists also use properties of matter to solve crimes.

Use your textbook and the ideas above to answer these questions.

6. Is the following statement true or false? Modern forensic science methods are completely different from those used by Archimedes.

_____

Name_____ Class_____ Date _____

7. What challenge did Archimedes face as he designed his experiment?

_____

_____

8. These silver and gold bars have the same mass but different volumes. Circle the letter of each statement that is true.

Silver
10.5 g/cm^3

a. Silver is about half as dense as gold.

b. The gold bar will displace more water than the silver bar.

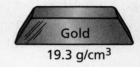
Gold
19.3 g/cm^3

c. Replacing some gold in a crown with silver will increase the volume of the crown.

9. Use the phrases in the box to complete the flowchart about analyzing paint.

detect energy	bombard with X-rays	identify elements

Analyze Paint

```
┌─────────────────────────────┐
│                             │
│                             │
│                             │
└─────────────────────────────┘
              │
              ▼
┌─────────────────────────────┐
│                             │
│                             │
│                             │
└─────────────────────────────┘
              │
              ▼
┌─────────────────────────────┐
│                             │
│                             │
│                             │
└─────────────────────────────┘
```

Lesson 1-2 Reading and Note Taking Guide

Securing and Recording a Crime Scene (pages 16–21)

Securing a Crime Scene (page 17)

Key Concept: Two ways to make a crime scene secure are to establish clear boundaries and limit entry to the crime scene.

▶ Sometimes people must rush into a crime scene to save a life or keep a suspect from escaping. Afterward, the police will secure the crime scene to prevent more damage.

▶ The police use yellow tape, ropes, or other objects to mark the boundaries of a crime scene.

▶ People who walk through a crime scene can leave objects behind by accident. These objects can cause confusion later when the team collects and tests evidence.

Use your textbook and the ideas above to answer these questions.

1. Read the phrases in the box. Which task does a police officer do first
   at a crime scene? _____

control entry
establish boundaries

2. How do investigators keep reporters away from a crime scene?
   Circle the letter of the best answer.

   a. They keep a log of all visitors.

   b. They tape off an area larger than the crime scene itself.

   c. They place seals on doors and windows.

3. Is the following statement true or false? Ideally, only members of the
   crime scene team should enter a crime scene. _____

4. List two things police do to control entry at a crime scene.

   _____

   _____

Name_____ Class_____ Date_____

Recording a Crime Scene (pages 18–21)

Key Concept: Investigators can use photographs, videos, sketches, and notes to make a record of a crime scene.

▶ Photographs show what a crime scene looks like before evidence is removed. Photographs are classified as long range, medium range, point of view, and close-ups.

▶ Videos show less detail than photographs but can provide a dramatic "you are there" experience for viewers.

▶ A **sketch** is a rough drawing that is done quickly and without much detail. A CSI will record measurements on the sketch. An artist uses the measurements to make a scale drawing. **Scale** is the ratio of a model to the actual size of an object.

Use your textbook and the ideas above to answer these questions.

5. Each type of photograph serves a different purpose. Draw a line from each type of photograph in Column 1 to a purpose in Column 2.

Type of Photograph	**Purpose**
long range	**a.** shows what a witness might see
medium range	**b.** focuses on the details of evidence
point of view	**c.** provides an overview of the crime scene
close-up	**d.** shows locations where there is evidence

6. The width of the windows in the scale drawing is 1/2 inch. What is the actual width of the window?

_____

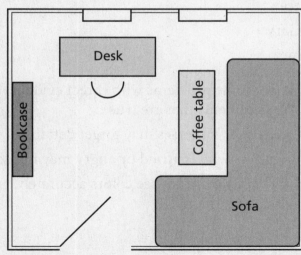

1/4" = 1 foot

Lesson 1-3 — Reading and Note Taking Guide

Types of Evidence (pages 24–31)

Direct Evidence (pages 24–25)

Key Concept: Some witnesses give accurate descriptions of what they saw or heard. But what a witness says is not always accurate.

▶ An eyewitness is a person who directly observes an event. The firsthand observations by eyewitnesses are **direct evidence**. This evidence can be used in court to prove a fact.

▶ Identifying witnesses is one of the first things police officers do at a crime scene.

▶ The descriptions that eyewitnesses give at a crime scene may not match. People's physical abilities, experiences, and emotions can affect their observations.

▶ Another problem with direct evidence is that witnesses may be asked to recall events weeks or months after they happen.

Use your textbook and the ideas above to answer these questions.

1. You and your friend Gary are in a store buying a magazine while your friend Inez waits outside. Suddenly you hear a screech of brakes and a crash as a car hits a fire hydrant. The police arrive. They ask, "Who can give us direct evidence about the crash?" Circle the letter of the correct choice.

   a. You

   b. Gary

   c. Inez

2. What are some problems with direct evidence? Circle the letters of all the statements that are true.

   a. Over time, witnesses may forget details.

   b. A witness who is afraid or angry may not see events clearly.

   c. Some people cannot see colors accurately.

Using Lineups and Mug Shots (pages 26–27)

Key Concept: Police may ask a witness to view a lineup or look at mug shots to help identify suspects.

▶ Lineups and mug shots are ways to help witnesses supply useful evidence. These methods are most useful when police have identified a suspect or the suspect has a criminal record.

▶ For a lineup to be fair, all the individuals in a lineup should be similar in appearance.

▶ Mug shots are photographs taken when a person is arrested. Witnesses may be asked to look at files of mug shots and pick out a suspect. Police may limit the search to criminals with a **modus operandi**, or MO, that fits the crime. A person's MO describes the way he or she approaches a task.

Use your textbook and the ideas above to answer these questions.

3. Is the following statement true or false? A lineup will always include the person who committed the crime. _____

4. Photographs taken from the front and side when someone is arrested are called _____.

5. Stealing red sports cars from mall parking lots between 8 P.M. and 10 P.M. on weeknights is an example of a(n) _____.

6. Look at the drawing of a lineup. Which person does not belong in the lineup and why?

_____

_____

Picturing a Criminal (pages 28–29)

Key Concept: Investigators can use sketches made by forensic artists to identify criminals. They can also use surveillance videos and facial recognition software.

▶ Working with witnesses, a forensic artist can make a reliable portrait of a suspect. The artist can draw sketches by hand or by using computer software.

▶ The cameras in banks, stores, and other public places are **surveillance cameras** (sur VAY luns). If a crime takes place within view of a surveillance camera, the camera records the action.

▶ There is computer software that can match a video image to an image in a database of mug shots. The software works by measuring distances between facial features.

Use your textbook and the ideas above to answer these questions.

7. Circle the letter of the method a forensic artist uses to make a sketch of a suspect.

   a. interviews eyewitnesses

   b. looks at a surveillance video

   c. uses facial recognition software

8. Why do some artists still prefer to make sketches by hand?

   _____

   _____

9. Complete the following sentences.

   a. If you see the sign "CCTV" in a bank or store, it means that there

   is a _____ at the location.

   b. Investigators can use _____ software

   to match images of faces.

10. Is the following statement true or false? It is easy to match an image recorded by a surveillance camera with a suspect's face.

   _____

Physical Evidence (pages 30–31)

Key Concept: Forensic scientists know that there is always a transfer of physical evidence at a crime scene.

▶ **Physical evidence** is any object than can be used to prove that a fact is true.

▶ Physical evidence may be found at a crime scene or in other locations related to the crime.

▶ French scientist Edmund Locard proposed an idea that is central to forensic science: Every contact leaves a trace.

▶ Criminals always leave some physical evidence at a crime scene. They always carry away some physical evidence from the scene.

Use your textbook and the ideas above to answer these questions.

11. A hair and flakes of skin are examples of _____ .

12. According to Locard's Principle, what causes evidence to be transferred at a crime scene? _____

13. A person struggles with an attacker. Circle the letter of an item that might be transferred during the struggle.

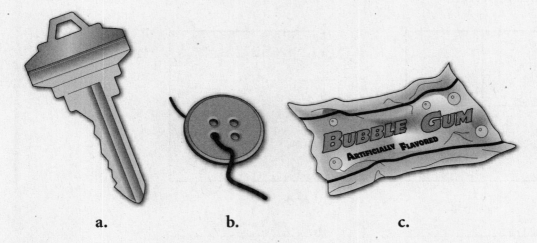

      a.   **b.**   **c.**

14. What influence did Locard have on the FBI?

_____

_____

Lesson 1-4 Reading and Note Taking Guide

Collecting Physical Evidence (pages 32–38)

Organizing a Search (page 33)

Key Concept: The team needs to consider the crime scene and pick a search pattern before they begin a search.

▶ The crime scene team must search in an organized way. If not, they are likely to miss some important pieces of evidence.

▶ Search patterns are designed to cover every inch of a crime scene. A team picks a search pattern based on the size of a crime scene and the size of the objects they are looking for.

Use your textbook and the ideas above to answer these questions.

1. Which type of crime scene needs to be searched quickly? Why?

_____

_____

2. The diagrams show two types of search patterns. Which drawing shows a grid search? Which shows a zone search? Write your answers on the lines provided.

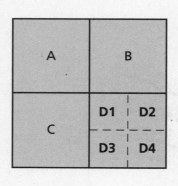   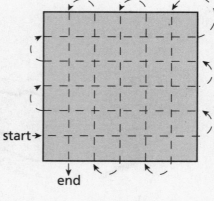

   a. _____   b. _____

3. In a line search, investigators move shoulder-to-shoulder across the crime scene. This pattern is useful in looking for a _____ object in a large area.

4. Is the following statement true or false? In a grid search, searchers cross the crime scene twice, but in different directions. _____

Name_____ Class _____ Date _____

Keeping Evidence Useful (pages 34–37)

Key Concept: Crime scene investigators must prevent contamination at the crime scene. They also must have the right equipment, package the evidence correctly, and keep a chain of custody.

▶ The adding of unwanted material to an object is called **contamination**.

▶ Investigators carry an equipment kit with tools for collecting different types of evidence.

▶ A CSI must choose the right container—paper bags, envelopes, plastic bottles—for packaging a piece of evidence.

▶ To make sure evidence can be presented in court, investigators must establish and maintain a **chain of custody**. This is a written record of who had control of a piece of evidence from the time it was collected.

Use your textbook and the ideas above to answer these questions.

5. Transferring sweat or oil from a hand to evidence is an example of

_____.

6. Draw a line from each piece of equipment in Column 1 to an example in Column 2 of how the equipment could be used.

Equipment

Purpose
a. to pick up bits of glass
b. to collect fingerprints
c. to look closely at a small object

7. What is the main reason investigators need to maintain a chain of custody? Circle the letter of the correct choice.
   a. They need to send the evidence to the lab for testing.
   b. They want to know who collected the evidence.
   c. They want to be able to use the evidence in a trial.

Name_____ Class_____ Date _____

Protecting the Investigators (page 38)

Key Concept: Crime scene investigators protect themselves by following established safety rules and procedures.

▶ People who work at a crime scene can be at risk from poisons, viruses, bacteria, sharp objects, and falling objects.

▶ At some crime scenes, a CSI adds a mask, goggles, and an extra pair of gloves. Protective clothing that is torn must be replaced.

▶ Some situations call for people with extra training.

Use your textbook and the ideas above to answer these questions.

8. Why is it unsafe for a CSI to eat her lunch at a crime scene? Circle the letter of the correct choice.

   a. Crumbs from her lunch may contaminate evidence at the scene.

   b. Harmful substances may enter her body through her mouth.

   c. She may be distracted from looking for evidence.

9. Draw a line to connect each situation in Column 1 with an appropriate safety procedure in Column 2.

Situation	Procedure
building damaged by fire	**a.** booties to cover shoes
muddy field	**b.** helmet and sturdy shoes
window smashed during a burglary	**c.** gloves

10. Describe a situation that would require people with extra training.

   _____

   _____

Lesson 1-1) Skills Lab

Who Stole Dave's MP3 Player?

Problem

What hypothesis can you develop about who stole your friend's MP3 player based on your review of the evidence?

Background

Investigators use scientific inquiry skills as they gather evidence at a crime scene. Their job is to find possible explanations for the evidence they collect. These explanations are called hypotheses.

In this activity, you will study various clues about a crime. Then you will develop a hypothesis about who committed the crime.

Skills Focus

observing, inferring, developing hypotheses

Procedure

At noon, your friend Dave goes to his locker and discovers that it is open. His MP3 player and his favorite pen are missing. So is a brown paper bag containing a sandwich and a large pretzel. Dave asks you to help him find the thief and the MP3 player before the end of the school day. To catch the thief, you need to interpret the data shown on pages 14 and 15 of your textbook.

Analyze and Conclude

1. **Observing** List two observations you can make from the illustrations on pages 14 and 15.

   _____

   _____

2. **Inferring** Based on where the brown paper bag was found, what can you infer about the thief?

   _____

   _____

Name_____ Class _____ Date _____

3. **Inferring** Think about the scrap of paper. What are two possible inferences you could make about the thief from this evidence?

_____

_____

_____

4. **Inferring** Why does Dave think the thief might be a girl?

_____

_____

5. **Interpreting Data** How would you use the fact that Dave's favorite pen is missing to help you catch the thief?

_____

_____

6. **Developing Hypotheses** Use your inferences to write a hypothesis about who stole Dave's MP3 player.

_____

_____

_____

Communicating

You have narrowed down the list of suspects to one or two students. You want the principal to search their lockers and backpacks for the MP3 player. Write a one-paragraph summary of the physical evidence and your inferences that will persuade the principal to take action.

_____

_____

_____

_____

_____

Lesson 1-2 ▸ Laboratory Investigation 1

Recording a Crime Scene

Problem

How can you record a crime scene?

Background

A janitor discovered drops of blood, a bloody hammer, keys, and other objects in a large storage room at the mall. The janitor told the store manager, who called the police. As a CSI, you know the importance of recording a crime scene before any evidence is removed. Your goal today is to photograph and sketch the crime scene.

Skills Focus

observing, inferring, making models, drawing conclusions

Materials

- numbered markers
- disposable film camera (or digital camera)
- evidence ruler
- graph paper
- metric ruler or tape measure
- poster board
- glue or tape

Safety First! 🖼

Use caution when walking around the crime scene to avoid tripping over objects. Do not touch anything in the crime scene.

Procedure
Part 1: Photograph a Crime Scene

The goal of photographing a crime scene is to make a detailed visual record of the scene before investigators disturb it.

1. Complete this step as a class. Take turns entering the crime scene and placing a numbered marker next to a piece of evidence. Use only the single path marked by the crime scene tape. Be careful not to disturb the evidence.

2. Break into teams to take turns photographing the crime scene. The first photo should be of the members of your team. Record the number and a brief description of each photo in the data table on page 19.

3. From outside the crime scene tape, take a long-range photo of the scene.

4. Move in a little closer and take three medium-range photos of the crime scene. Take each photo from a different angle or location.

5. Enter the crime scene. Take a close-up photo of each piece of evidence. Make sure the numbered marker is included in each close-up photo. For smaller objects, include the evidence ruler in the photo. Be careful not to disturb the evidence when you place the evidence ruler.

6. When you are finished, your teacher will show you how to print your photos or will print them for you.

Part 2: Display Your Photographs

In this part of the lab, you will organize, display, and label your photos.

7. Work with your team. Use the information in the data table to organize your photos. Glue or tape your photos onto a piece of poster board. Leave room beneath each photo to make notes. Study the details in each photo and think about what inferences you could make based on your observations. Write your inferences in the space below each photo.

Name_____ Class _____ Date _____

Part 3: Sketch a Crime Scene

A crime scene sketch is a record of the most important details of a crime scene.

8. On a separate sheet of paper, sketch the boundaries of the crime scene. Measure the length and width of the scene. Record the measurements on your sketch.

9. Sketch the location of each piece of numbered evidence. Include other objects in the crime scene that might provide a frame of reference for the evidence.

10. Make measurements to record the location of each object. You may need to measure the distance of an object from the edge of the crime scene or from the path.

11. Compare your sketch with the sketch from another team. Are there different objects in the sketches? Discuss any differences and decide if you want to add or erase objects from your sketch.

Data Table		
Number	**Type**	**Description of photograph**
1	team photo	
2	long-range	
3	medium-range	
4	medium-range	
5	medium-range	
6	close-up	
7	close-up	
8	close-up	
9	close-up	
10	close-up	
11	close-up	
12	close-up	
13	close-up	
14	close-up	
15	close-up	

Analyze and Conclude

1. Why do you think investigators place numbered markers next to evidence at the crime scene?

   _____

   _____

   _____

2. The evidence is visible in the medium-range photos. Why did you also need to take close-up photos of the evidence?

   _____

   _____

3. Review your crime scene photos. Describe how you might use the photos later in an investigation.

   _____

   _____

   _____

4. Select three objects you included in your sketch. Explain why you selected these objects and how you think the objects would be helpful in an investigation.

   _____

   _____

   _____

5. In this investigation, you took long-range, medium-range, and close-up photos. You also made a sketch of the crime scene. What are some other ways to record a crime scene?

   _____

   _____

Communicating

Write a short note to another CSI. Include any tips you learned about photographing a crime scene.

_____

_____

_____

Lesson 1-3 Laboratory Investigation 2

Making Faces

Problem

How can you use computer software to make a sketch of someone's face?

Background

A forensic artist works with an eyewitness who can provide firsthand observations of an event. These observations are direct evidence. Some police departments have computer software that forensic artists use to create sketches of people, based on eyewitness descriptions. In this activity, you will play the role of a forensic artist. Your goal will be to create a sketch based on someone else's description.

Skills Focus

observing, communicating

Materials

- computer (PC or Macintosh)
- printer
- face-sketching software
- photographs of people
- poster board

Procedure

Part 1: Learn to Use the Software

You will learn how to use the face-sketching software by playing a game called "Observation Exercise." A face will appear on the screen for several seconds. During this time, observe the face and try to remember as many details as possible. Then use the software to sketch the face.

1. Click the Start Observation Exercise button (the icon shaped like an eye at the top of the screen). Select 1 for the level of difficulty. At the bottom of the setup screen, change the viewing time from 4 to 10 seconds. Click Start Exercise. When the sample face appears, study the features. Observe hairstyle, head shape, eye shape, eyebrows, nose, lips, jaw shape, and facial hair.

2. When the sample face disappears, use the Features Palette on the right side of the screen to sketch the face. Click on the type of facial feature you want to sketch. A limited number of choices are available in game mode. If you select a type of feature and no choices appear, move on to another type of feature. Select the shape or style that best matches the sample face. Continue until you have sketched the sample face as accurately as possible.

3. When you are finished, click the Stop Observation Exercise icon. The original sketch and your sketch will appear side-by-side. Compare the original with your sketch. What features match? What features do not match? Are there any features you forgot to include?

4. Show the summary screen to your teacher. Then, click OK. The summary screen will disappear and the software will return to its opening screen.

5. Repeat this exercise four more times. As you become more familiar with the software, increase the difficulty level. Your goal is to identify different categories of facial features and then find those features in the software. You want your sketches to be as close to the original face as possible.

Part 2: Interviewing an Eyewitness

A forensic artist must interview an eyewitness to get a description of a suspect. In this part of the activity, you will sketch a face based on a description from an eyewitness.

6. Decide with your partner who will be the eyewitness and who will be the forensic artist. The eyewitness selects a photograph of a person. The eyewitness must not show the photo to the forensic artist.

7. The forensic artist should interview the eyewitness by asking questions about specific facial features. The eyewitness should answer the artist's questions based on the facial features in the photograph. As the eyewitness describes each feature, the artist should select the feature from the software that best matches the description.

8. When the sketch is complete, print it out and compare it with the original photograph. Decide with your partner what changes could be made to make the sketch as accurate as possible. Give the sketch and the photo of the person to your teacher.

9. Switch roles and repeat the activity.

10. When everyone in the class has sketched a person, your teacher will display all the sketches. Look at each sketch and locate the photo that most closely matches the sketch. Record the number of the sketch and the name of the person in the data table.

11. After all students have finished Step 10, your teacher will tell you which photo belongs with each sketch. Pick a sketch and decide how you might improve it to better represent the actual person.

Data Table			
Sketch	Person's name	Sketch	Person's name

Analyze and Conclude

1. How can the sketch of a suspect help police during an investigation?

   _____

   _____

2. What are the benefits of using computer software instead of pencil and paper to make a sketch?

   _____

   _____

3. A suspect may try to change her appearance to escape detection. How can a forensic artist make a sketch that will help police locate a suspect even after a suspect changes her hair color and style?

   _____

   _____

4. What problems did you have when you tried to sketch the face described by your partner?

   _____

   _____

   _____

5. In what ways is the procedure in Part 2 similar to what a forensic artist experiences when making a sketch?

   _____

   _____

   _____

Communicating

Select one of the photos and study it. Record the person's name. Write a sentence or two that accurately describes the person's facial features.

_____

_____

_____

_____

Name_____ Class_____ Date_____

Lesson 1-4 — Laboratory Investigation 3

Collecting Physical Evidence

Problem

How would you collect physical evidence from a crime scene?

Background

The crime scene has been recorded. The next step is to collect the physical evidence. Any object that can be used to prove that a fact is true is considered physical evidence. You must be careful not to contaminate the evidence during the collection process. You must also protect yourself and other investigators from being injured by objects from the crime scene. As soon as the evidence is collected, you must start the chain of custody log.

Skills Focus

classifying, controlling variables, drawing conclusions

Materials

- 2 pairs of tweezers
- paper evidence bags
- plastic evidence bags
- cotton swab with tube
- evidence tags
- chain of custody log
- booties (optional)
- head coverings (optional)

Safety First!

Wear plastic gloves. Your teacher may provide booties, head coverings, and lab aprons. If so, put booties on over your shoes, a head covering on your head, and the lab apron over your clothes. Use caution when you walk around the crime scene. Booties can be slippery on tile floors. Wash your hands thoroughly with soap and warm water after you have completed the activity.

Name_____ Class_____ Date _____

Procedure

1. Discuss with your teammates your strategy for collecting the evidence you have been assigned. Decide which tools you will use and which containers to use to store the evidence.

2. Wear gloves and any other protective clothing available. With your partner, make sure you have no loose threads or hairs hanging from your clothes that could fall off and contaminate the crime scene.

3. Gather the tools and collection containers you will use and bring them to the crime scene. If tweezers are required, use one pair of tweezers for each item of evidence you will collect. Throw away the tweezers after each use to prevent contaminating evidence.

4. Collect the evidence and place it in the proper storage container.

5. Fill out the appropriate information on the storage container. If you are using a small container, fill out the information on an evidence tag. Attach the tag to the container.

6. Fill out the chain of custody log for the evidence you collected. Deposit the collected evidence in the location specified by your teacher.

7. After you have collected your evidence and left the crime scene, remove and dispose of booties, gloves, and head coverings. Return lab aprons to your teacher. Then, wash your hands thoroughly with soap and warm water.

Analyze and Conclude

1. Give two reasons why it is necessary for investigators to wear plastic gloves while collecting evidence from a crime scene.

_____

_____

_____

2. How many items should be stored in each evidence container? Why?

_____

_____

3. Why is it important to seal any container holding physical evidence?

_____

_____

_____

_____

4. Why is it important to have a complete and accurate chain of custody for evidence?

_____

_____

5. Describe everything that a CSI does to keep evidence useful for a trial.

_____

_____

_____

_____

Communicating

Assume that you looked at a chain of custody log and there was a period of time on the log when the evidence was not accounted for. Explain what might have happened to the evidence during that time.

_____

_____

_____

_____

Chapter 1) Chapter Project

Investigating a Crime Scene

Background

In this activity, you will begin solving the Missing Masterpiece mystery. The crime scene for this mystery is shown on page 1 of your textbook. Drawings of 36 suspects with facts about each person are on pages 2 and 3. You will use these facts to help solve the crime.

   Here is what is known so far. Police were called to a Main Street mansion early this morning. A woman reported hearing an alarm and seeing a car speed out of the driveway. When police entered the house, they noticed that a painting was missing. Police also noticed several objects of evidence that may provide clues about who stole the painting.

Skills Focus

observing, inferring, posing questions, making models

Your Goals

Using the information found in Chapter 1 and the drawing on page 1, you will

- observe, describe, and sketch the crime scene

- prepare questions to interview the eyewitness

- identify evidence at the crime scene

Procedure

Part 1: Make Observations and Inferences

To make an observation, you use one or more of your senses to gather information. When you make an inference, you offer a reasoned opinion based on your observations and experience.

1. Examine the drawing on page 1 of your textbook. In Column 1 of Data Table 1, write observations about the crime scene. In Column 2, write an inference that is based on each observation in Column 1.

Name_____ Class_____ Date _____

Data Table 1	
Observation	Inference

Name_____ Class_____ Date _____

Part 2: Secure the Crime Scene

Two ways that investigators secure a crime scene are to mark clear boundaries and to limit entry to the crime scene.

2. Examine the drawing. List all the areas that are part of the crime scene.

_____

_____

_____

3. How would you protect the footprints and broken glass evidence in this crime scene?

_____

_____

_____

Part 3: Sketch the Crime Scene

Investigators use photographs, videos, sketches, and notes to record the details of a crime scene.

4. Make a sketch of the crime scene. Include all the indoor and outdoor details that you think are important. The placement of objects in the sketch should reflect their locations in the crime scene.

Name_____ Class _____ Date _____

Part 4: Interview an Eyewitness

Witnesses provide direct evidence about a crime. Sometimes witnesses will give accurate descriptions of what they saw or heard. But witnesses are not always accurate. Investigators need to ask the right questions to learn as much as possible from witnesses.

5. A woman was walking her dog near the Main Street mansion. She saw a car speed out of the mansion's driveway. Prepare a list of five questions you would ask when interviewing this eyewitness.

Question 1: _____

Question 2: _____

Question 3: _____

Question 4: _____

Question 5: _____

Part 5: Identify Physical Evidence

Physical evidence is any object that can be used to prove that a fact is true.

6. In Data Table 2, list items of physical evidence. Include a description of each item's location.

Data Table 2	
Physical Evidence	Location

Name_____ Class _____ Date _____

Analyze and Conclude

1. What is the difference between an observation and an inference?

   _____

   _____

   _____

2. What steps would police take when they first arrived at the Main Street mansion crime scene?

   _____

   _____

   _____

3. When you made a sketch of the Missing Masterpiece crime scene, how did you decide which objects to include and which to ignore?

   _____

   _____

   _____

4. What advice would you give to an eyewitness who observed a crime? What advice would you give to an investigator who is interviewing an eyewitness?

   _____

   _____

   _____

   _____

5. Apply Locard's principle to two items of physical evidence you identified at the Missing Masterpiece crime scene.

   _____

   _____

   _____

   _____

Communicate

Make a poster that describes the first steps that should be taken when a CSI arrives at a crime scene. Use sketches to illustrate your poster.

Chapter 1) Video Viewing Guide

Clues From a Murder

1. According to the video, what three main factors did detectives rely on 200 years ago to solve crimes?

_____

_____

2. Why do you think the sheriff chose Toms as a suspect?

_____

_____

3. How did the investigators connect Toms to the crime? What inquiry skill did they use?

_____

_____

_____

4. Why do investigators secure a crime scene?

_____

_____

5. List two pieces of evidence that modern investigators might have looked for at the crime scene.

_____

_____

6. List three pieces of evidence that modern investigators might have collected from the suspect.

_____

_____

_____

7. List three inquiry skills that investigators use to solve crimes.

_____

_____

The Mysterious Ice Man

8. Why did scientists infer that the Ice Man was murdered?

_____

_____

9. Describe the experiment the scientists did to test their hypothesis that the Ice Man was a shepherd who climbed the mountain as he herded goats and sheep.

_____

_____

_____

10. What were the results of the experiment and what did the scientists conclude from these results?

_____

_____

_____

Interviewing Witnesses

11. What does an interviewer want from an eyewitness?

_____

12. Describe what often happens during a standard interview.

_____

_____

13. Describe what happens during a cognitive interview.

_____

_____

_____

14. Which interview technique is more effective? Why?

_____

_____

Chapter 2 Building Science Vocabulary

Words With Multiple Meanings

Many words in English have multiple meanings. This is true for some terms used in forensic science. To understand what you are reading, you need to be aware of these multiple meanings. Look for the words in the table below as you read this chapter.

Word	Everyday Meaning	Meaning in Forensic Science
concentration	*n.* Close or fixed attention on a task or idea **Example:** His sister started yelling at the dog, which broke his <u>concentration</u> on his math homework.	*n.* The amount of one substance in a given mass or volume of a mixture **Example:** The tea had a high <u>concentration</u> of sugar.
impression	*n.* An effect produced, on the mind or senses, by something or someone **Example:** I had a good <u>impression</u> of the movie based on the coming attractions.	*n.* The pattern left when an object is pressed into a surface **Example:** Her shoe left an <u>impression</u> in the wet cement.

Apply It!

Read the sentences. Decide which meaning of the underlined word is being used—the everyday meaning or the scientific meaning. Write your choices on the lines provided.

1. The <u>concentration</u> of gold is lower in 14-karat gold than in 18-karat gold.

   _____

2. The new student wanted to make a good <u>impression</u>.

   _____

3. The truck tires left deep <u>impressions</u> in the snow.

   _____

Name_____ Class_____ Date _____

Building Science Vocabulary (continued)

Greek Word Origins

Many modern scientific terms are made up of word parts that come from Ancient Greek words. For example, *telephone* comes from the Greek word parts *tele*, meaning "far off," and *phone*, meaning "sound." The table below lists some other Greek word parts that can be combined to form scientific terms.

Word Part	Meaning	Example
chroma-	color	**chromium** element named for its brightly-colored compounds
-graphy	method for writing or recording	**biography** a written record of a person's life
micro-	small	**microsecond** one millionth of a second
-scope	an instrument for seeing or observing	**telescope** instrument designed to observe objects that are far away

Apply It!

Use the information above to answer the following questions.

1. What is a microscope?

   _____

   _____

2. Chromatography is a method used to separate a mixture based on the properties of its components. What property of matter is contained in the name of this method?

   _____

3. The Greek word part *photo-* means "light." Use the meanings of the word parts *photo-* and *-graphy* to define the word *photography*.

   _____

   _____

Name_____ Class _____ Date _____

Prints (pages 44–51)

Types of Prints (pages 45–47)

Key Concept: Investigators look for imprints and impressions made by objects that leave a distinctive pattern.

▶ **Prints** are marks left when an object is pressed against the surface of another object. Flat prints with only two dimensions are called **imprints**. Prints that have three dimensions—length, width, and depth—are called **impressions**.

▶ From an impression of a shoe, print examiners can detect shoe size, the pattern on a sole, and unique wear patterns.

▶ The part of the tire that touches the road is called the tread. Print examiners can use marks and wear patterns on tire treads to connect a specific tire to an impression.

▶ A **skid mark** is the mark left when a vehicle with locked wheels slides along a road surface.

▶ Print examiners also examine the marks left by tools and gloves.

Use your textbook and the ideas above to answer these questions.

1. Why are marks left by shoe soles and tire treads extremely useful as evidence? Circle the letter of the correct choice.

   a. Marks left by these items are common at crime scenes.

   b. Shoes and tires leave both imprints and impressions.

   c. Shoe soles and tire treads have distinctive patterns.

2. Draw a line from each term in Column 1 to the correct description in Column 2.

Term	**Description**
impression	**a.** mark left when car slides across a road
imprint	
skid mark	**b.** print with only two dimensions
tool mark	**c.** mark left by the blade of a chisel
	d. pattern pressed into a soft surface by an object

3. Is the following statement true or false? Wearing gloves ensures that a criminal cannot be linked to a crime. _____

Name_____ Class _____ Date _____

Preserving Prints (pages 48–49)

Key Concept: Investigators can preserve prints by taking photographs, making casts, or removing objects from a crime scene.

▶ A photographer can use lighting to capture every possible detail when taking photographs of an impression. The photographer takes a series of photos of skid marks or a trail of muddy shoe prints.

▶ Investigators can make a cast of an impression. A **cast** is an object made by filling a mold with a liquid that takes the shape of the mold as it changes to a solid.

▶ Investigators may send both tools and objects with tool marks to the lab for examination. They may also make casts of tool marks.

Use your textbook and the ideas above to answer these questions.

4. Why does a photographer place a light at a low angle near an impression?

_____

_____

5. Why does a photographer place a ruler near an impression?

_____

6. Use the words in the box to complete the paragraph below.

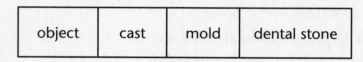

object	cast	mold	dental stone

An impression can act as a _____. A CSI

pours _____ into the impression.

The _____ that forms when the liquid sets

can be compared to the _____ that made

the impression.

7. Is the following statement true or false? The best way to match a tool with a tool mark is to try to fit the tool into the mark.

_____

Comparing Prints (page 50)

Key Concept: Forensic scientists use computer databases to identify and compare prints. They also compare prints found at a crime scene to objects that belong to a suspect.

► Most databases are organized sets of computer records. A print examiner can scan an image of a print and add a record for the print to a database. Then the examiner can search for similar records in the database.

► A print examiner also can compare a print made from an object to a print found at a crime scene.

Use your textbook and the ideas above to answer these questions.

8. Complete the graphic organizer about shoe print databases.

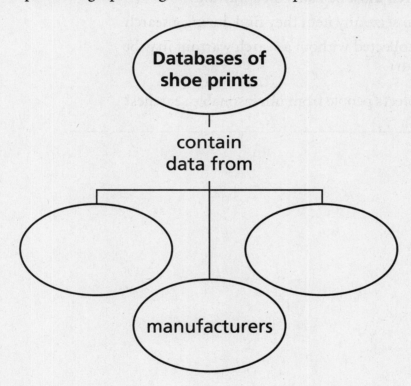

9. Investigators have a suspect's shoe and a print from a crime scene. What should they do next? Circle the letter of the correct choice.

   a. Make a print of the shoe.

   b. Make an impression of the shoe.

   c. Make a cast of the shoe.

Search Warrants (page 51)

Key Concept: A search warrant protects a suspect's rights and ensures that a search is legal.

▶ A **search warrant** is a written court order that allows police to search for specific objects at a given time and place. The warrant allows police to seize property as evidence.

▶ To get a warrant, police have to show that their planned search is reasonable. They must explain why they expect to find evidence of a crime during a search.

Use your textbook and the ideas above to answer these questions.

10. Circle the letter of each statement that is true.

   a. The time of a search must be listed on a warrant.

   b. Police officers can seize any item they find during a search.

   c. Evidence that is collected without a search warrant may be thrown out in court.

11. What document protects people from unreasonable searches?

   _____

Lesson 2-2 · Reading and Note Taking Guide

Trace Evidence (pages 54–61)

Collecting Trace Evidence (page 55)

Key Concept: To collect trace evidence, investigators need to know where to look. They also must have the right tools.

▶ Tiny amounts of physical evidence that are transferred at a crime scene are called **trace evidence**.

▶ Investigators must find trace evidence before they can collect it.

▶ A CSI uses tools such as tweezers, tape, or a vacuum to collect trace evidence.

Use your textbook and the ideas above to answer these questions.

1. Is the following statement true or false? Even after a crime scene is cleaned, there is probably trace evidence at the crime scene.

   _____

2. Which of these tools would be most useful for collecting a hair caught in a watchband? Circle the letter of the correct choice.

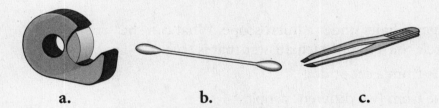

a.   b.   c.

Types of Trace Evidence (pages 56–59)

Key Concept: Five major groups, or types, of trace evidence are hair, fibers, paint, glass, and soil.

▶ Hairs have three layers: a cuticle, a cortex, and a medulla. Hairs can be used to narrow a list of suspects. Hairs can't be used to positively identify a suspect because many people have hair with a similar structure.

▶ Fibers are long, slender strands that can be woven or knitted together. Natural fibers, such as cotton, come from animals or plants. Synthetic fibers, such as polyester, are developed in labs.

▶ Paint is a mixture, meaning that its composition can vary. There is a database of paint samples called the Paint Data Query, or PDQ. It contains test results for hundreds of thousands of paint samples.

Name_____ Class_____ Date_____

▶ A scientist can measure the concentration of elements in a sample of glass. **Concentration** is the amount of a substance in a given mass or volume of a mixture.

▶ Scientists often can match a soil sample to a specific location. They look at properties such as color, size of particles, and pollen.

Use your textbook and the ideas above to answer these questions.

3. Use the words in the box to label the diagram of a hair.

cortex	cuticle	medulla

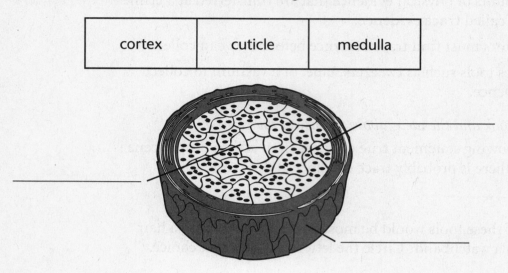

4. An examiner compares hairs under a microscope. What can she know for sure? Circle the letter of each answer that is true.
   a. if the hairs came from a cat or dog
   b. if the hairs came from two different people
   c. if the hairs came from the same person

5. Complete the following sentences. Fibers that come from plants and animals are _____ fibers. Fibers that are developed in labs are _____ fibers.

6. Is the following statement true or false? Paint chips can be used to identify the make and model of a car. _____

7. Why do scientists look at seeds and pollen in a soil sample? Circle the letter of the correct choice.
   a. The composition of soil does not vary.
   b. Every soil sample contains seeds and pollen.
   c. Seeds and pollen often come from specific locations.

Using Chromatography (page 60)

Key Concept: Trace evidence is often a mixture. So a forensic scientist needs a way to separate mixtures.

▶ There are tests that a forensic scientist can use to positively identify a substance. These tests work best when the substance being tested is not mixed with other substances.

▶ **Chromatography** (kroh muh TAHG ruh fee) is one way to separate mixtures based on their properties. The size of the different particles in a mixture affects their speed.

Use your textbook and the ideas above to answer these questions.

8. Is the following statement true or false? Chromatography is the only method used to separate mixtures. _____

9. Why do the particles in a mixture separate during gas chromatography? Circle the letter of the correct choice.

    a. Particles of different substances move at different speeds.

    b. The particles exist as gases at higher temperatures.

    c. Some of the particles can absorb light.

Using Microscopes (page 61)

Key Concept: With a microscope, scientists can see details of evidence that are not visible to the unaided eye.

▶ A **microscope** is an instrument that makes very small objects look larger.

▶ Forensic scientists use microscopes to identify and compare evidence.

▶ To magnify tiny traces many hundreds of times, scientists use a scanning electron microscope (SEM).

Use your textbook and the ideas above to answer these questions.

10. What can a scientist do with a comparison microscope?

_____

11. Is the following statement true or false? Some microscopes use electrons to produce an image. _____

Lesson 2-3　Reading and Note Taking Guide

Identifying Firearms (pages 64–68)

Evidence From Firearms (pages 65–66)

Key Concept: Investigators look for the evidence that is left behind when a weapon is fired. Firing a gun leaves impressions on a cartridge case and on a bullet. Firing a gun leaves trace evidence on the person who fires the gun.

▶ A bullet is packed in a metal case called a **cartridge**. A cartridge also contains gunpowder and a primer.

▶ Pulling a trigger on a gun causes a firing pin to strike the cartridge. This pressure causes the primer to ignite, which in turn ignites the gunpowder. The hot gases produced by the reaction push the bullet through the barrel of the gun at high speed.

▶ A distinctive mark is left on a cartridge when the firing pin strikes the cartridge.

▶ Inside a gun barrel, there are spiral grooves called **rifling**. The grooves leave marks on a bullet that match the size, spacing, and angle of the grooves.

▶ Often, some of the gunpowder and primer in a cartridge does not burn. This material is called **gunshot residue**.

Use your textbook and the ideas above to answer these questions.

  1. Use the words in the box to label the contents of a cartridge.

primer	gunpowder	bullet

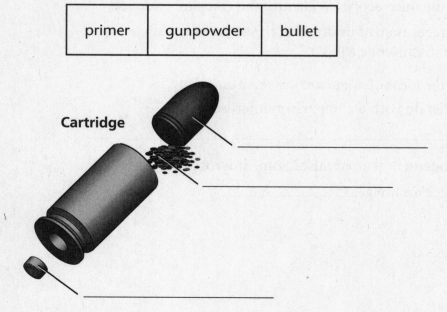

Cartridge

_____

_____

_____

2. Which object leaves a mark on a cartridge when a gun is fired? Circle the letter of the correct choice.

   a. trigger

   b. hammer

   c. firing pin

3. What leaves marks on a bullet when a gun is fired? Circle the letter of the correct choice.

   a. trigger

   b. rifling

   c. firing pin

4. Is the following statement true or false? The location of bullets can be used to trace a path back to the spot where a gun was fired.

   _____

5. Circle the letter of the trace evidence found when a gun is fired.

   a. a dent left by a firing pin

   b. scratches on a bullet

   c. gunshot residue

Analyzing Firearms Evidence (pages 67–68)

Key Concept: Microscopes and chemical tests are used to check for gunshot residue. Microscopes and databases are used to compare impressions from firearms.

▶ Under a microscope, some particles of gunshot residue have a distinctive shape. Investigators can also use chemical tests to identify elements in gunshot residue.

▶ An analyst will test fire a bullet from a gun to compare with a bullet from a crime scene. The analyst can use a comparison microscope to see if the bullets have the same pattern of scratches.

▶ A technician can search a database to match firearms evidence from one crime to evidence from other crimes.

Use your textbook and the ideas above to answer these questions.

6. Is the following statement true or false? Gunshot residue contains traces of lead, barium, and antimony. _____

7. If two bullets have the same rifling, what does a firearms analyst know for sure? Circle the letter of the correct choice.

   a. The bullets were fired from the same type of gun.

   b. The bullets were fired from the same gun.

   c. The bullets were fired by the same person.

8. How does a technician begin to search for a match in a firearms database?

   _____

   _____

9. List two advantages of using a database of firearms evidence.

   _____

   _____

   _____

   _____

Lesson 2-1 Skills Lab

Analyzing Shoe Prints

Problem

How can you match an unknown shoe print to a specific shoe in a shoe print database?

Background

Someone tried to break into the file cabinet in the principal's office. The file cabinet contains answer keys to the end-of-year exams. The only evidence left in the office was a muddy shoe print. It is your job to find out who attempted the break-in.

In this activity, you will make and analyze a print of your own shoe. Your teacher will use the prints you and your classmates make to create a shoe print database. Finally, your teacher will provide you with a copy of the shoe print from the principal's office. It will be your job to see if you can match that print with any of the prints in the database.

Skills Focus

observing, measuring, calculating, classifying

Materials

- plastic gloves
- apron
- washable black ink
- felt pad
- plastic tray
- large sheet of plain white paper
- newspaper
- metric ruler
- transparency grid
- transparent tape
- dry erase marker
- database of shoe prints

Safety First!

Wear plastic gloves and an apron to prevent ink from getting on your hands and clothes. Wash your hands immediately after the activity.

Name_____ Class _____ Date _____

Procedure
Part 1: Making Shoe Prints
The goal of this part of the activity is to make a clear print of the bottom of your right shoe.

1. Spread newspaper over the area on the floor where you and your partner will be making prints.
2. Place the felt pad in the plastic tray. Spray or pour washable black ink evenly over the surface of the felt pad.
3. Step carefully into the plastic tray with your right foot. While your shoe is in contact with the felt pad, gently rock your foot back and forth a few times. This motion will distribute the ink evenly over the sole of your shoe. Be careful not to get ink on the sides or top of your shoe or on your socks or pants.
4. Step from the tray directly onto the middle of the white paper. Don't rock your foot back and forth or turn it in any way.
5. Lift your foot straight up from the white paper and walk to the sink. Be sure to walk only on the newspaper.
6. Remove your shoe. Use the materials at the sink to clean the ink off the bottom of the shoe.

Part 2: Analyzing a Shoe Print
The goal of this part of the activity is to analyze a shoe print.

7. Once the print is completely dry, use a metric ruler to determine the total length and width of the print. Record the measurements in your data table.
8. Use the shoe size conversion chart to determine the approximate size of your shoe. Record the shoe size in your data table.
9. Place a transparency grid over the print. Line up the top of the grid with the top of the print. Center the grid, left to right, over the print. Tape the grid in place over the print. Then use the marker to draw an outline of the print on the grid.

Foot Length to Shoe Size Conversion Chart

Length (cm)	22.8	23.1	23.5	23.8	24.1	24.5	24.8	25.1	25.4	25.7	26	26.7	27.3	27.9	28.6	29.2
Men	3½	4	4½	5	5½	6	6½	7	7½	8	8½	9	10½	11½	12½	14
Women	5	5½	6	6½	7	7½	8	8½	9	9½	10	10½	12	13	14	15½

10. Carefully examine the print under the grid. Identify any marks in the shoe sole, such as nicks and cuts. Draw these marks on the grid. Also note any places where the sole is worn down. Then record your observations in your data table. Be sure to include the location of each mark (A1, C12, and so on).

Part 3: Matching a Shoe Print

The goal of this final part of the activity is to match an unknown shoe print with one of the prints in a shoe print database.

11. Your teacher will assemble all the prints into a database. Your teacher will also give you a shoe print that was found at the scene of the crime. Use the database to find a match for the print.

Data Table		
Feature	**Observation or Measurement**	
Length of print (cm)		
Width of print (cm)		
Shoe size		
Marks on shoe sole	**Grid Box**	**Observation**

Name_____ Class _____ Date _____

Analyze and Conclude

1. **Designing Experiments** Look at the database of prints. Are there prints that are smeared? Are some prints incomplete because ink was not spread evenly on the sole? Suggest two ways to change the procedure in Part 1 to reduce these problems.

_____

_____

2. **Calculating** What would the shoe size be for a man's shoe with a length of 27.6 cm? What would the size be for a woman's shoe?

_____

_____

3. **Interpreting Data** Explain why it would be important to line up the print and the grid in the same way for every print.

_____

_____

4. **Classifying** Describe the steps you followed to match the print your teacher gave you with a print in the database.

_____

_____

5. **Drawing Conclusions** Assume a CSI was able to match a shoe print from a crime scene to a shoe belonging to a suspect. Using only the shoe print evidence, what conclusion could the CSI reach?

_____

_____

_____

Communicating

Write a paragraph comparing the steps you used to analyze a shoe print to the steps a print examiner might use in a crime lab.

_____

_____

_____

_____

_____

Lesson 2-1) Laboratory Investigation 4

Casting Suspicion

Problem

How can you make a cast of a tire tread impression?

Background

Someone has damaged the high school football field by driving on it. There were no eyewitnesses, but fresh tire impressions were left in the soil on the field. Police made a cast from the impression. Then they compared the cast to tires on vehicles in the school parking lot. In this activity you will use a similar process to make a cast of a tire impression. Then you will use the cast to match the impression to the correct tire tread.

Skills Focus

controlling variables, making models, drawing conclusions

Materials

- plastic tray
- loam
- metric ruler
- graduated cylinder, 100-mL
- spray bottle
- plastic spoon
- tire tread section
- hair spray
- casting powder
- casting frame
- craft stick
- laboratory scoop
- toothbrush

Safety First

Wear goggles, a lab apron, and plastic gloves. Do not spray others with water from the spray bottle. Do not spray hair spray toward anyone. Hair spray is flammable; do not use it near an open flame. If a plastic bag with casting powder in it breaks, do not inhale the dust. If casting mixture spills on the floor, do not step on it because it will be slippery. Wipe up any water on the floor immediately. Wash your hands thoroughly with soap and water after the activity.

Procedure
Part 1: Making a Tire Impression

1. Put on goggles, a lab apron, and plastic gloves. Spread enough soil over the bottom of the plastic tray so that the soil is 2 cm deep. Break up any clumps of soil.

2. Use a graduated cylinder to measure 50 mL of water. Pour the water into a spray bottle. Spray the surface of the soil evenly and then use your fingers or a plastic spoon to stir the soil. Repeat spraying and stirring until all the water is mixed into the soil. Spread the soil evenly over the bottom of the tray.

3. Obtain a tire tread section from your teacher. Place the tire section, tread pattern down, onto the dampened soil. Press down firmly and evenly so the entire tread surface is pressed into the soil. Be careful not to move the tire section sideways or twist it while you are pressing down.

4. Lift the tire tread up slowly so you don't damage the impression. Return the tire tread to your teacher. Take care not to bump into or move the plastic tray because this could damage the tire impression.

5. Use hair spray to help preserve the impression. Hold the hair spray bottle about 20 cm away from the impression. Spray the impression evenly with one coat of hair spray.

6. Open the plastic bag that contains casting powder. Use a graduated cylinder to slowly pour 250 mL of water into the bag. Squeeze out most of the air and reseal the bag. Then mix the powder and water together by gently squeezing the bag. Handle the bag gently so it does not break.

7. Place the casting frame around the impression and gently push it into the soil. Slowly pour the casting mixture onto the soil near the impression. Let the mixture flow into the impression. To avoid damaging the impression, do not pour the mixture directly into the impression. Make sure the mixture entirely fills the impression.

8. Allow the mixture to set for 15 minutes. Select one team member to use a craft stick to gently carve initials into the top surface. Allow the mixture to set overnight.

Part 2: Comparing a Tire Cast With Tire Treads

9. When the mixture is solid, carefully lift the cast out of the soil. Turn it over and use a laboratory scoop and toothbrush to clean away as much soil as possible. Do not use a lot of force because you might chip off part of the cast. Make sure the soil falls back into the tray. Use running water and the toothbrush to finish removing soil from the cast.

10. Use paper towels or cloths to gently dry your cast. The cast is fragile, so use caution not to break it.

11. Your teacher has displayed different tire tread sections and labeled each of them. Take your cast to the display and match your cast with the proper tire tread.

_____

Analyze and Conclude

1. How do the ribs on a tire tread appear in an impression of the tire?

   _____

   _____

2. Why would it be easier to compare a tire tread to a cast of the tire than to an impression of the tire?

   _____

   _____

   _____

   _____

3. Is the tire tread cast an exact copy of the tire tread? What are the similarities between the cast and the tread? What are the differences?

   _____

   _____

   _____

   _____

   _____

4. The police made a cast to investigate what caused the damage to the football field. Print examiners matched the cast to a tire on a vehicle in the school parking lot. What conclusion could they reach based solely on that match?

_____

_____

_____

_____

5. Getting good results when making a cast takes skill and experience. Which steps in the procedure did you find most challenging? Why?

_____

_____

_____

Communicating

Write a story for the school newspaper that describes what happened at the football field. Explain how police used evidence to find the car that might be responsible. Describe the steps that investigators used to make a cast of the tire tread impression.

_____

_____

_____

_____

_____

_____

_____

Lesson 2-2 Laboratory Investigation 5

Splitting Hairs

Problem

Can you identify which hair samples are human?

Background

There was a break-in at a local animal clinic. People working at the clinic reported that valuable lab equipment and animals are missing. Investigators searched the crime scene and collected hair samples. Detectives have asked investigators to determine if any of the hair samples are human.

In this activity, you will prepare two types of microscope slides: a cuticle-impression slide and a whole-mount slide. A cuticle-impression slide shows the scale patterns on the cuticle. A whole-mount slide enables you to view the medulla. After you make the slides, you will observe the hair samples under the microscope. Your goal is to answer the detectives' question: Are any of the samples human hair?

Skills Focus

observing, classifying, drawing conclusions

Materials

- black construction paper
- copy paper
- hair samples
- microscope slides
- clear fingernail polish
- plastic forceps
- grease pencil
- slide-mounting solution
- cover slips
- microscope

Safety First! 🖐 ♻ 🚫 🔥 🧤

Wear plastic gloves. Do not breathe the fumes from the fingernail polish or slide-mounting solution. Do not use fingernail polish near a flame. Follow your teacher's instructions when you use the slide-mounting solution. Be careful when you focus the microscope that the lens does not touch the slide. Slides and cover slips are fragile, and the lens can break the slide. If a slide breaks, tell your teacher. Wash your hands with soap and warm water immediately after the activity.

Procedure

Part 1: Preparing Hair Sample Slides

In this part of the activity, your team will make a cuticle-impression slide and a whole-mount slide of one of the hair samples.

1. Your teacher will give you an envelope with hair samples. Make sure your work area and tools are clean and the area is well lit. Tape a piece of white copy paper onto one half of a piece of black construction paper. Use the appropriate black or white background to help you see the individual strands of hair you are handling.

2. To make a cuticle-impression slide, apply a thin coat of clear fingernail polish to a clean slide. Use forceps to place two hairs on the polish while the polish is still wet. After 45 seconds, use forceps to remove the hair.

3. Use a grease pencil to label the slide with the same label that is on the hair-sample envelope. Do not place anything on top of your cuticle-impression slide or the impression will be damaged.

4. To make a whole-mount slide place a drop of mounting solution in the center of a clean slide. Use forceps to place two hairs onto the drop of mounting solution. Do not get mounting solution on the forceps. Place the hairs next to each other. Do not let the strands overlap. Place a cover slip on top of the drop of mounting solution. Use forceps to press down gently on the cover slip to spread the mounting solution. (CAUTION: Pressing down on the cover slip with too much force will break the cover slip.)

5. Label the slide with the same label that is on the hair-sample envelope. Do not view the slide under the microscope until the mounting solution is completely dry.

6. Place the finished slides on a tray set aside by your teacher in the storage area.

Part 2: Analyzing Hair Samples

In this part of the activity, you will observe and identify the characteristics of each hair sample.

7. Refer to Appendix B: Using a Microscope on pages 152–153 of your textbook. Review the procedures for using a microscope.

8. Select one of the cuticle-impression slides and place it on the microscope stage. Record the slide label in the first column of the data table.

9. First view the cuticle impression under low power. Then view the impression under high power. There are three different cuticle shapes shown in Figure 1. Which sketch best represents the pattern you see in the impression? Record the shape of the cuticle in your data table.

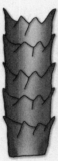  

Crown   Leaf   Scale

10. Return the slide to the storage area and select another cuticle-impression slide. Repeat Steps 8–9 until you have observed all six cuticle-impression slides.

Data Table			
Hair sample	Cuticle shape	Medulla thickness	Medulla shape

Name_____ Class _____ Date _____

11. Select one whole-mount slide and place it on the microscope stage.

12. View the hair sample under low power and then under high power. Does the hair have a medulla? If so, observe the thickness of the medulla compared with the thickness of the hair. If the medulla takes up less than half of the hair's diameter, then the medulla is thin. If the medulla takes up more than half of the hair's diameter, then it is thick. If you do not see a medulla at all, then it is absent. Record the thickness of the medulla in the data table. Be sure to use the row in your data table that matches the label on the whole-mount slide.

13. Observe the medulla again. Look at the sketches of different medulla shapes in Figure 2. Which sketch best represents the medulla shape for the hair you are viewing? Record the shape of the medulla in the data table. If you do not observe a medulla, write *absent*.

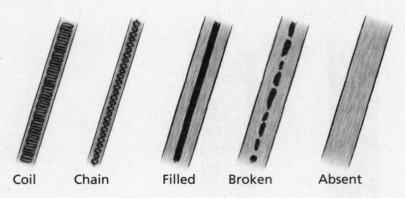

Coil   Chain   Filled   Broken   Absent

14. Return the slide to the storage area and select another whole-mount slide. Repeat Steps 12–13 until you have observed all six whole-mount slides.

Name_____ Class_____ Date_____

Analyze and Conclude

1. Describe the difference between a cuticle-impression slide and a whole-mount slide. What structures of a hair are best seen in each type of slide?

   _____

   _____

   _____

2. What three characteristics can be used to tell the difference between human hair and animal hair?

   _____

3. Human hairs have scale-shaped cuticles. Which hair samples had scale-shaped cuticles?

   _____

4. Human hairs have thin medullas. Which hair samples had thin medullas?

   _____

5. The medullas of human hairs can be filled, broken, or absent. The medullas of some animal hairs have definite shapes, such as a chain or coil. Which hair samples had filled, broken, or absent medullas? Which hair samples had medullas that looked like coils or chains?

   _____

   _____

   _____

6. An operational definition defines the characteristics of an object. Write an operational definition that could be used to identify human hair.

   _____

   _____

   _____

   _____

Name_____ Class_____ Date _____

Communicating

Write a lab report that would be helpful to detectives. Describe the methods you used to observe the hair samples. Also, include a brief description of how you determined which samples were human.

_____
_____
_____
_____
_____
_____
_____
_____

Lesson 2-2   Laboratory Investigation 6
Lipstick Tells the Tale

Problem

How can lipstick be used as evidence that a suspect was at a crime scene?

Background

A reporter at a large newspaper was working on a story about a politician who was accepting bribes. The reporter left her desk during lunch. When she returned to her desk, she noticed some papers were missing. The missing papers had information about the story she was working on.

The only evidence left behind was a coffee mug with lipstick on it. Neither the mug nor the lipstick belonged to the reporter. The police questioned the reporter. The reporter suggested three possible suspects: the politician's campaign manager, a rival reporter, and the politician's wife.

Investigators collected a sample of the lipstick from the mug. That lipstick was labeled X. They also collected lipstick samples from the suspects and labeled them A for the manager, B for the reporter, and C for the wife.

In this activity, you will use chromatography to compare lipstick from the mug with the lipstick samples from the suspects. Lipstick is made by mixing different color pigments to obtain the desired color. Each color pigment in the mixture should move across the chromatography paper at a different speed. As a result, the lipstick samples may show different bands of color even though the shades are similar.

Skills Focus

observing, measuring, calculating, classifying

Materials

- chromatography paper
- pencil
- metric ruler
- scissors
- lipstick
- cotton swabs
- alcohol solution
- graduated cylinder, 25-mL
- glass jar with lid
- plastic forceps

Safety First! 🫁 ✋ 🧥 🚱 ☣️ ⚠️ 🧤 🧴

Goggles, gloves and an apron must be worn when working with the alcohol solution. The alcohol solution is a poison. Do not breathe it in or taste it. Use it only in a well-ventilated area. If any solution is spilled, tell your teacher immediately. Alcohol should not be used near a flame. Handle glass items with care. Do not apply lipstick on skin or lips. Use cotton swabs only as directed by your teacher. Wash your hands with warm water and soap immediately after the activity.

Procedure

1. Put on the goggles, lab apron, and plastic gloves. Obtain one piece of round chromatography paper.

2. Crease the paper by gently folding it in half and opening it up again.

3. On the crease in the paper, make one small pencil mark 2.5 cm from the edge of the paper. Make another small pencil mark on the crease 3.5 cm from the edge.

4. Use a ruler to draw a faint pencil line perpendicular to the crease that intersects the 3.5-cm pencil mark. This is the base line. Draw a second faint pencil line at the 2.5-cm mark. When you are finished, you should have two faint parallel pencil lines, as shown in the figure below.

5. Use scissors to cut along the 2.5-cm line to create a flat edge across the bottom of the paper.

6. Use a pencil to write the letters A, B, C, and X about 2 cm below the top edge of the paper. Make sure the letters are evenly spread across the width of the paper. Write your team name above the letters.

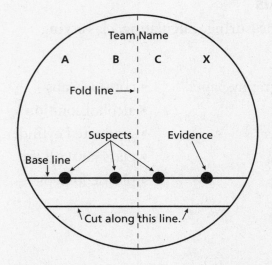

7. Obtain a swab with a lipstick sample from your teacher. The swab will be labeled. Use the swab to carefully place a spot of lipstick on the base line. The spot should be directly under the letter that matches the letter on the swab label. The lipstick spot should be an even circle about 0.5 cm in diameter. Make sure there are no clumps in the lipstick spot.

8. Repeat Step 7 with the other lipstick samples.

9. Bring your chromatography paper to the area containing the jars. Be careful not to smear or contaminate the lipstick samples.

10. Pour 15 mL of alcohol into the graduated cylinder. Pour the alcohol into the glass jar.

11. Carefully refold the chromatography paper along the crease into a V-shape. Be careful not to let the lipstick spots touch each other as you refold the paper. You do not want to smear or contaminate the samples. The paper must fit inside the jar without touching the sides of the jar and stand on its bottom edge with no additional support.

12. Place the paper into the jar so that the straight edge is parallel to the bottom of the jar as shown in the figure below. Be sure the lipstick spots remain above the level of the alcohol in the jar at all times.

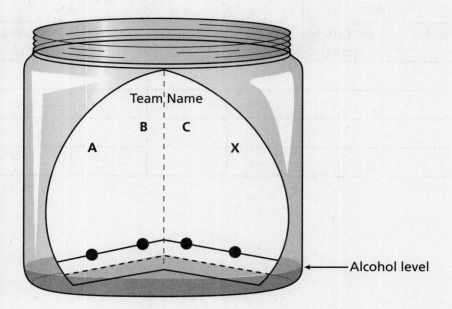

13. Screw the lid onto the jar and leave the jar undisturbed for 30–35 minutes. The alcohol will rise up the paper. Remove the lid when the alcohol level reaches the letters at the top of the paper.

14. Use plastic forceps to remove the chromatography paper from the jar. Allow the paper to dry completely in a well-ventilated area designated by your teacher.

15. Observe the results. Working from the bottom up, identify the color bands above each sample. Record each band in the data table.

16. Use a pencil and ruler to mark the highest position of each color band.

17. Measure the distance between the highest position of each band and the baseline. Record the distances, in centimeters, in the data table.

18. Tape your chromatography paper in the display space indicated by your teacher.

19. Dispose of the alcohol according to your teacher's directions. Do not pour the alcohol down the drain. All other materials may be put in the trash.

Data Table							
A		B		C		X	
Color	Distance (cm)	Color	Distance (cm)	Color	Distance (cm)	Color	Distance (cm)

Name_____ Class_____ Date_____

Analyze and Conclude

1. What evidence do you have that the lipsticks were mixtures?

   _____

   _____

2. Which lipstick sample had the most number of color bands? Which sample had the least number of color bands?

   _____

   _____

   _____

3. Which lipstick from a suspect is most similar to the lipstick from the crime scene?

   _____

   _____

   _____

   _____

   _____

4. Based only on the lipstick analysis, what conclusion can you draw about the suspect whose lipstick matched the lipstick from the crime scene? Can this evidence alone be used to prove that the suspect stole the papers?

   _____

   _____

   _____

   _____

   _____

5. What do you think detectives would do next after they receive the results of the lipstick analysis?

_____

_____

_____

Communicating

Write a report for the detectives who are investigating this crime. Summarize your laboratory findings. Be sure to describe how the lab results showed which suspect had lipstick similar to the lipstick on the mug.

_____

_____

_____

_____

_____

_____

Lesson 2-2 Laboratory Investigation 7

A Clear-Cut Case

Problem

How can microscopes, cameras, and computer images be used to compare and match physical evidence samples?

Background

A cheerleading championship trophy was stolen from the trophy case at school. In its place, the thief left a ransom note. The note was torn out of a small, spiral notebook, but a corner of the page is missing.

Detectives collected notebooks from three suspects. All three notebooks have page corners left in the notebook. You will use a digital camera and digital imaging software to compare the ransom note with similar page corners from the three different notebooks. Then you will decide which notebook the note came from.

The school has a burglar alarm, but the thief cut the copper wires leading to the alarm. Detectives found three types of tools in the suspects' lockers. You will examine the cut wires using a digital camera attached to a microscope and digital imaging software. You will compare the tool marks on the cut alarm wires with sample marks made by the three different tools. Then you will decide which tool was used to cut the alarm wires.

Skills Focus

observing, inferring, drawing conclusions

Materials

- page corner evidence
- digital camera
- computer
- Motic® Trace software
- microscope
- cut wire evidence

Safety First! ✂

Follow all instructions that your teacher gives you. The camera, computer, and microscope are delicate instruments and must be handled with care. Handle the copper wire pieces with care, as the ends may be sharp.

Procedure
Part 1: Matching Paper Corners

Detectives labeled small corners of paper from three note-books S-1, S-2, and S-3. Your job is to see if any of these corners are from the ransom note.

1. Obtain a ransom note and set of torn page corners from your teacher.

2. Open the Motic Trace software. Click File>New>Live Video>OK. Center the paper corner labeled S-1 under the camera. Make sure the entire torn edge is in view. Focus the image by turning the focusing ring on the CCD lens a small amount. Then wait for the image to refresh on the screen. Continue this process until the paper corner is in sharp focus.

3. Click File>Auto Capture. Make sure the *Use Current Time* box is not checked. Enter S-1 in the *File Name* box. Select *.jpg* as the file type. Set *Capture Interval* to 1 Second; set *Total Image* to 1. Click OK. The software will capture the still image of the paper corner and save it to your *Pictures:Motic Library* folder. The file name will be S-1.jpg.

4. Remove the S-1 paper corner. Center the S-2 paper corner under the camera and repeat Step 4. Enter S-2 as the *File Name*. This new image file name will be S-2.jpg.

5. Center the S-3 paper corner under the camera and repeat Step 4. Use S-3 as the *File Name*.

6. Position the evidence paper so the missing corner is centered under the camera. Repeat Steps 3–4, except the *File Name* will be Evidence.

7. Close the live camera window and click File>Open. Select the four images you just made and open them.

8. Use Evidence.jpg as the base, or bottom, image. You will place each corner image on top of the base image. One image placed on top of another is called an overlay.

9. Select the S-1.jpg image. Click and hold on the circle to the left of the file name at the top of the image window. Drag the S-1 image into the Evidence image window and release the mouse button. The S-1 corner image is now layered on top of the Evidence image.

10. Select Tools>Show Info. As you drag the slider to the left, the corner image will become more and more transparent. When the slider is in the middle, click Set as Default. Now the rest of your overlays will become semi-transparent as soon as you drag them over the base image.

11. Line up the page corner with the missing corner in the evidence image. You may need to reduce or enlarge the size of the overlay image by clicking on one of the red circles at a corner of the top layer and dragging the corner in or out. If necessary, rotate the overlay image. You can do this by clicking on the edge of the top layer and dragging it in the direction you want to rotate.

12. When you have lined up the corner image and the Evidence image, save the result as a combined image. Click File>Capture Image. Name the file ComboS-1.jpg.

13. Remove the S-1 image by clicking File>Delete. The top layer will be deleted.

14. Repeat Steps 9–13 with S-2.jpg and S-3.jpg. The file names of the combined images should be ComboS-2.jpg and ComboS-3.jpg.

15. Close the paper corner and evidence files. Open the three combo images. Arrange them on the screen next to each other, or print them out so you can compare them.

Part 2: Comparing Tool Marks

A print examiner made sample cuts in copper wire using the three tools found in the suspects' lockers. Using a microscope, digital camera, and image software, you will compare the sample cuts with the cut alarm wires.

16. Attach the camera to a microscope, plug the camera into the computer, and open the Motic Trace software.

17. Obtain three cards with wires from the suspects' tools and one card with evidence from the crime scene.

18. Rotate the low-power objective lens into place. Put the card labeled S-1 on the microscope stage so a cut end of the wire is visible.

19. Click File>New>Live Video>OK. Move the card until the cut end of the wire is in the center of the field of view. Use the microscope focusing controls to focus the image. Focus a little at a time and wait for the image to refresh on the screen.

20. Follow the instructions for making and saving combination images from Part 1. You will photograph the three wire samples and the wire from the crime scene. Then you will overlay the images, photograph the combined images, and print them for comparison.

Analyze and Conclude

1. Which notebook corner most likely came from the ransom note? Explain how you reached that conclusion.

   _____

   _____

2. Based on the results of your comparison can you definitely conclude that the ransom note came from a particular notebook. Why?

   _____

   _____

3. Which of the three tools is easiest to distinguish by the shape it leaves on the wire, and why?

   _____

   _____

   _____

4. Which tool most likely cut the alarm wires? Explain.

   _____

   _____

   _____

5. What advantages are there to using a digital camera and software to observe evidence?

   _____

   _____

Communicating

Write a brief report that summarizes your investigation. Explain how you compared each sample with evidence from the crime scene.

   _____

   _____

   _____

   _____

   _____

Chapter 2) Chapter Project

Analyzing Print and Trace Evidence

Background

Investigators found a ransom note and tire tracks at the "Missing Master-piece" crime scene. Later, the detectives were allowed to collect pens from the suspects and make prints of the tires on the suspects' cars. In this activity, you will analyze physical evidence to narrow the list of 36 suspects. In Part 1, you will make tire prints from sections of tire tread. The tire tread matches the tires that made prints at the crime scene. You will then use the prints to identify the brand of tire from a tire brand data-base. In Part 2, you will use paper chromatography to analyze ink from the ransom note. Your goal is to identify the brand of pen used to write the note.

Skills Focus

observing, classifying, drawing conclusions

Your Goals

Using evidence and photographs provided by your teacher, you will

- make a tire print from a tire tread
- use paper chromatography to analyze ink
- match your samples with images in a database

Materials

Part 1
- newspaper
- felt pad
- plastic tray
- ink
- graduated cylinder
- spray bottle
- tire tread section
- white paper

Part 2
- filter paper
- filter paper with ink sample
- scissors
- graduated cylinder
- metric ruler
- small plastic cup
- stopwatch or clock
- graph paper

Safety First 🖐️ 🧤 ✋ 🔥

Wear goggles, a lab apron, and plastic gloves. Wipe up any spills. Black ink can stain skin and clothing. Wash hands thoroughly with soap and water when you finish each part of this activity.

Procedure

Part 1: Making Tire Prints

Detectives know the brand of tire on each suspect's car. Identify the brand of tire found at the crime scene and you will narrow the list of suspects.

1. Put on goggles, a lab apron, and plastic gloves. Spread newspaper over the area where you and your team will be making tire prints.

2. Place the felt pad in the plastic tray. Pour 120 mL of black ink into the spray bottle and spray the ink evenly over the surface of the felt pad.

3. Obtain a tire tread section from your teacher. Place the tire tread on the felt pad (tread side down). Press the tread evenly into the felt pad to distribute ink over the entire surface of the tread.

4. Lift the tread section straight up from the felt pad. Gently touch the inked tire tread to a piece of newspaper to remove excess ink. Then, press the tire tread firmly and evenly onto a clean piece of white paper. Do not twist or turn the tire tread section, as this motion will smear the print. Lift the tire print straight up from the paper.

5. Examine the print. If the print is smeared, repeat Steps 3–4 with the same tire tread to make a new print.

6. When you have a clean print, carry the tire tread to the sink. Use soap and water to wash the ink off the tire tread. Rinse out the graduated cylinder and spray bottle. Be careful not to splash water and ink outside the sink.

7. Write one name from the team at the top of the paper above your tire print. Allow the print to dry overnight.

8. Throw away newspapers in the trash. Return the cleaned tire tread section to your teacher.

Part 2: Analyzing Ink Using Paper Chromatography

A forensic scientist used paper chromatography to analyze ink from each brand of pen owned by the suspects. The results are posted in the classroom. The scientist also isolated the ink from the ransom note for you to test. Identify the brand of pen used to write the ransom note and you will narrow down the list of suspects.

9. Fold a piece of filter paper in half twice. The folded piece should look like a piece of pie. Unfold the paper and use scissors to cut along the fold lines. When you are done, you should have four pie-shaped pieces of paper.

10. Roll one of the pie-shaped pieces into a cone shape and set it aside.

11. Obtain a folded piece of inked filter paper from your teacher. The ink is from the ransom note.

12. Open the inked filter paper and lay it flat on your desk. On each of the fold lines, place a pencil mark 1 cm from the edge of the filter paper. There should be four pencil marks when you are finished.

13. Refold the inked filter paper in half twice. Use scissors to carefully cut a 2-mm or 3-mm curved piece from the tip of the folded paper. Unfold the paper. You should have a nearly circular hole in the middle of the ink. Make sure there is still a border of ink at least 3 mm wide surrounding the hole in the filter paper.

Twice-folded filter paper

Ink

Cut line should be curved

14. Hold the inked paper ink side up. Insert the narrow end of the cone-shaped filter paper through the hole from below. When you are done, the small end of the cone should be sticking up between 1 cm and 2 cm above the ink. About 5 cm to 8 cm of the cone should extend down from the inked filter paper. You now have a filter paper assembly.

15. Use a graduated cylinder to measure 50 mL of water and pour the water into a plastic cup. Place the filter paper assembly on the rim of the cup. Make sure the bottom of the paper cone is below the surface of the water. Add more water if you need to. NOTE: The water must not touch the inked filter paper, just the bottom of the cone. Also, make sure the cone is touching the entire inside edge of the inked circle. In Data Table 1, record the time that you put the filter paper assembly into the water.

16. The water will rise up the cone and slowly spread across the inked filter paper. Every 5 minutes, measure the distance between the outer edge of the ink and the edge of the hole in the filter paper. Keep the filter paper assembly on the cup as you measure the ink. Record the results in Data Table 1. Also, record any additional observations you make about the colors and patterns you observe.

17. Let the chromatography continue until the outer edge of ink reaches the pencil marks on the fold lines.

18. Remove the filter paper assembly from the cup. Remove the cone from the filter paper. Set the inked filter paper aside to dry.

19. Pour the water from the plastic cup into a sink and rinse the cup. Return the plastic cup to your teacher. Discard the paper cone in the trash. Save the inked filter paper.

Data Table 1		
Starting time:		
Time (min)	Distance traveled (mm)	Observations
5		
10		
15		
20		
25		
30		

Analyze and Conclude

1. Compare your tire print to the tire brand database. Which tire tread photograph is the best match with your tire print? Tell your teacher the code under that photograph and your teacher will tell you the brand name of that tire. Write that brand name in all 12 rows of Data Table 2.

2. Refer to the list of suspects on pages 2–3 of the textbook. In Data Table 2, record the names of the 12 suspects whose cars have this brand of tire. Also record the pen brand for each of those suspects.

Data Table 2		
Tire Brand	**Suspect's Name**	**Pen Brand**

3. On a sheet of graph paper, use the data in Data Table 1 to draw a line graph. Use Time (min) for the *x*-axis and Distance Ink Traveled (mm) for the *y*-axis. Study the graph and write a one-sentence summary that describes how the outer edge of ink progressed during the time you observed it.

_____

_____

_____

4. Examine the color pattern from your ink chromatography results. Starting from the center of the filter paper, list the colors that you observe.

_____

_____

5. Compare the results of your ink chromatography with the sample results posted in the classroom. What brand of pen was used to write the ransom note? In Data Table 2 draw a line through the names of suspects who do not own that brand of pen. What are the names of the remaining suspects?

_____

_____

Communicate

Write a brief paragraph to summarize the tests you did in this activity. Describe how you used your results to narrow the list of suspects from 36 to 4. Be sure to include the names of the remaining suspects.

_____

_____

_____

_____

_____

_____

_____

_____

Chapter 2) Video Viewing Guide

Tire Tracks Trap Killer

1. What two methods are used to preserve tire track evidence?

   _____

   _____

2. How did the tire track expert identify the brand of tire that made the impressions at the crime scene?

   _____

   _____

   _____

3. Investigators were able to obtain tires from a truck to compare with the prints from the crime scene. Summarize the process they used to do the comparison.

   _____

   _____

   _____

   _____

4. Would tire tread evidence alone be enough to convict a suspect? Why or why not?

   _____

   _____

Arson-Sniffing Dogs

5. What evidence do fire investigators look for to prove that a fire was set on purpose?

   _____

   _____

6. When a dog detects an accelerant what does the arson investigator do with the sample, and why?

   _____

   _____

   _____

7. What did the forensic chemist discover when he tested the sample from the crime scene?

_____

_____

8. What makes dogs so helpful to arson investigators?

_____

_____

_____

9. In the experiment the scientists did with the dogs, what was the variable? What do the scientists use as controls? What conclusion did they draw from the data?

_____

_____

_____

_____

Firearms Evidence

10. What causes striations on a bullet? Why are these marks useful in identifying firearms?

_____

_____

_____

_____

11. Why are test bullets fired into a tank of water?

_____

_____

12. What tool does a firearms analyst use to observe and compare the marks on bullets?

_____

13. What information can be inferred from studying the pattern of gun-shot residue on a victim's clothing?

_____

_____

Chapter 3 | Building Science Vocabulary

High-Use Academic Words

High-use academic words are words that are used frequently in class-rooms. You and your teachers use these words when you discuss topics in science and other subjects. Look for the words in the table below as you read this chapter.

Word	Definition	Sample Sentence
eliminate (ee LIM uh nayt) pp. 78, 83, 99	*v.* to remove from a list or group; to get rid of; to no longer consider	People with food allergies may need to eliminate shellfish, eggs, or wheat from their diet.
initial (ih NISH ul) pp. 81, 83	*adj.* coming first or present at the beginning of an event or process	Her initial reaction to winning the contest was to jump up and down.
reliable (rih LY uh bul) p. 81	*adj.* can be counted on; can be trusted to be accurate or to provide a correct result	Read the volume in a graduated cylinder at eye level to get a reliable measurement.
reveal (rih VEEL) pp. 76, 77, 98	*v.* to make known something that is hidden (or secret)	The stage manager drew back the curtain to reveal the set for Act I of the play.
unique (yoo NEEK) pp. 74, 75, 92	*adj.* being the only one of its kind	The designer promised to make a unique dress for the actress to wear to the award show.

Apply It!

Choose the word that best completes each sentence.

1. The analyst used a hand lens to do an _____ exam of the print.

2. Every chemical element has a _____ atomic number.

3. After Josh checked the prices for athletic shoes, he had to _____ a few models from his list of favorites.

4. The detectives decided that the witness had not given them _____ evidence.

Building Science Vocabulary (continued)

Using Related Word Forms

You can increase your vocabulary by learning related forms of a word or words with the same root. For example, suppose you know that *fragile* means "easily broken." You can guess that a *fragment* is a piece left when something is broken. The table shows words that are related to some Key Terms from Chapter 3.

Key Term	Meaning	Related Words
visible print *n.*	a fingerprint that can be seen	**vision** *n.* the ability to see; sense of sight **invisible** *adj.* not able to be seen **visibility** *n.* the distance it is possible to see under the existing conditions
probability *n.*	a measure of the chance that an event will happen	**probable** *adj.* likely to exist or happen **improbable** *adj.* not likely to happen **probably** *adv.* most likely; to be expected
endangered species *n.*	a species whose numbers are so small that it may disappear from the world	**danger** *n.* risk; something that may cause injury or damage **dangerous** *adj.* unsafe; likely to result in harm **endanger** *v.* to expose to danger; to threaten with extinction

Apply It!

Review the meanings of visible *and related words. Choose the correct word to complete the following sentences.*

1. A thick fog reduced the _____ at the airport.

2. Harry Potter has a cloak that can make him _____.

3. A microscope can reveal details that are not _____ to the unaided eye.

Lesson 3-1   Reading and Note Taking Guide

Fingerprints (pages 74–79)

Describing Fingerprints (page 75)

Key Concept: There are three typical patterns of ridge lines—loops, whorls, and arches.

▶ No two people, not even identical twins, have the same fingerprints.

▶ On your fingertips, there is a series of raised lines, or **ridges**. These ridges make the lines you see on your fingerprints.

▶ Print examiners look for both the overall pattern and the details that make a print unique.

Use your textbook and the ideas above to answer these questions.

1. Draw a line from each term in Column 1 to the correct description in Column 2.

Ridge Pattern	Description
loop	**a.** The lines form a circle around a central point.
whorl	**b.** There is a series of curved lines, one above the other.
arch	**c.** The lines start on one side and curve back, like the bend in a river.

2. Use the words in the box to label the diagram of a fingerprint.

dot	enclosure	fork	ridge ending

3. Is the following statement true or false? Only identical twins have the same fingerprints. _____

Collecting Fingerprints (pages 76–77)

Key Concept: Methods that are used to reveal and improve latent prints include dusting, chemical reactions, and lighting.

▶ Fingerprints found at a crime scene are rarely complete or clear. They are often hard to see.

▶ A **visible print** is a print that can be seen. A **plastic print** is an impression left in a soft material.

▶ When you transfer sweat or oil from the ridges of your fingers to the surface of an object, you leave a hidden print, or **latent print**.

▶ A CSI can dust for latent prints on hard surfaces with a fine powder. For porous surfaces, which can absorb sweat and oil, scientists use chemical reactions to reveal latent prints.

▶ A forensic photographer can use white light to make prints stand out or use powders that glow when they are exposed to UV light.

▶ Once a print is visible, a CSI uses transparent tape to "lift," or remove, the print from a surface.

Use your textbook and the ideas above to answer these questions.

4. What kind of print is left by a finger wet with blood? Circle the letter of the correct choice.

   a. visible print

   b. plastic print

   c. latent print

5. How could you reveal latent prints on a doorknob?

   _____

6. How could you reveal latent prints on a ransom note?

   _____

   _____

7. How could you reveal latent prints on a leather wallet?

   _____

8. Is the following statement true or false? Dusted prints that are lifted are placed on a card with a contrasting color. _____

Identifying Fingerprints (pages 78–79)

Key Concept: Fingerprint examiners first try to eliminate some prints. Then they try to match the remaining prints with those of a suspect or with prints in a database.

▶ A crime scene is likely to contain more fingerprints than those left by the person who did the crime. A print examiner needs to eliminate those prints as evidence.

▶ Print examiners first identify the ridge pattern of a print. Then they look at details, such as forks, and small variations.

▶ An examiner can use the FBI database to compare prints. The computer searches for possible matches. The print examiner looks at the images and decides whether there is a match.

Use your textbook and the ideas above to answer these questions.

9. Why do police collect fingerprints from people who are not suspects?

_____

10. What is the correct sequence for comparing fingerprints? Use the phrases in the box to complete the flowchart.

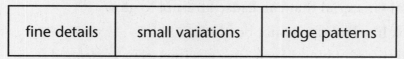

| fine details | small variations | ridge patterns |

Comparing Fingerprints

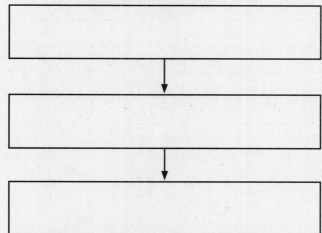

11. Circle the letter of each statement about AFIS that is true.

    a. Finding a match with AFIS saves time.

    b. Investigators don't need a print examiner.

    c. Investigators have more data.

Lesson 3-2 Reading and Note Taking Guide

Evidence From Blood (pages 80–85)

Searching for Blood (page 81)

Key Concept: Some chemicals produce light or change color in the presence of hemoglobin. The chemicals can be used to detect or test for blood at a crime scene.

▶ Blood is a water-based mixture with cells suspended in the water. Red blood cells consist mainly of a molecule called **hemoglobin** (HEE muh gloh bin), which carries oxygen to cells in the body.

▶ A CSI uses ultraviolet light or sprays luminol on surfaces where he or she suspects there is blood. **Luminol** emits a blue glow when it comes in contact with blood.

▶ Tests done at the crime scene must be confirmed by other tests in the lab.

Use your textbook and the ideas above to answer these questions.

1. Circle the letter of each statement that is true.

   a. Blood is the only material that can cause luminol to glow.

   b. Stains that look like blood may not be blood.

   c. A CSI can find traces of blood even after a crime scene is cleaned.

2. What method can a CSI use to test a stain that is visible?

   _____

   _____

   _____

   _____

Classifying Blood (pages 82–83)

Key Concept: Scientists can use antibodies to classify blood.

▶ Human blood can be classified into four major groups, or types. These types are A, B, AB, and O. The groups are named after marker molecules found on the surface of red blood cells.

▶ **Antibodies** are molecules that bind to marker molecules. Each antibody will bind to one specific molecule.

▶ Blood cells with A marker molecules clump when mixed with Anti-A antibodies. Blood cells with B marker molecules clump when mixed with Anti-B antibodies.

▶ Blood types cannot be used to identify a suspect, but they can be used to reduce the number of suspects.

Use your textbook and the ideas above to answer these questions.

3. The table lists four blood types and two antibodies that could be mixed with each type of blood. Complete the table by writing "clumps" or "does not clump" in the unfilled boxes to show what happens when each blood type is mixed with Anti-A or Anti-B antibodies.

Data Table		
Blood Type	**Anti-A**	**Anti-B**
O		
A		
B		
AB		

4. Why can't investigators use blood type to identify a suspect? Circle the letter of the correct choice.

a. Blood typing is not an accurate process.

b. Many people have the same blood type.

c. Chemicals used to detect bloodstains can change the blood type.

Bloodstain Patterns (pages 84–85)

Key Concept: Investigators analyze patterns of bloodstains to figure out what happened at a crime scene.

▶ The shape of a bloodstain depends on the distance that the blood traveled and the angle at which it hit the surface.

▶ Blood that is sent flying by a blow will break into smaller drops when it hits a surface. The size of the drops is used to estimate the force of the blow.

▶ The tip of a bloodstain always points in the direction that the blood had been moving.

▶ A space in the middle of a blood spatter pattern is a clue that an object was present at the time of the attack.

Use your textbook and the ideas above to answer these questions.

5. A bloodstain is round with ragged edges. Circle the letter of each statement that is true.

   a. The blood hit the surface at a 90-degree angle.

   b. The blood hit a soft or porous surface.

   c. The blood fell a short distance.

6. Complete this sentence. The size of blood drops _____ as the force of a blow increases.

7. Look at the drawing of blood spatter below. In which direction was the blood traveling when it hit the surface? Explain your answer.

   _____

   _____

   _____

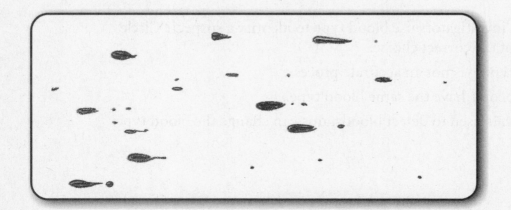

Lesson 3-3 — Reading and Note Taking Guide

DNA Evidence (pages 88–95)

DNA Molecules (page 89)

Key Concept: Except for identical twins, no two people have nuclear DNA with the exact same sequence of base pairs.

▶ **DNA,** or deoxyribonucleic acid (dee ahk see ry boh noo KLEE ik), is the molecule that carries traits from parents to offspring.

▶ **Proteins** are molecules that your body uses to build tissues and organs. Proteins also control the chemical reactions that take place in cells.

▶ DNA is found in the nucleus of body cells.

▶ In a DNA molecule, two long strands are coiled around each other. The strands are connected by weak chemical bonds between pairs of nitrogen bases, or base pairs.

▶ A **gene** is a section of DNA that contains information your cells need to make a protein. The order of the bases in a gene is a code that determines which protein is produced.

Use your textbook and the ideas above to answer these questions.

1. Circle the letter of each statement about DNA that is true.

   a. DNA controls the production of proteins.

   b. DNA in muscle cells is different from DNA in skin cells.

   c. A DNA molecule looks like a twisted ladder.

2. Is the following statement true or false? Nuclear DNA is a combination of the DNA a person inherits from each parent.

   _____

3. The drawing below shows a section of DNA. One base in each base pair is labeled. Use the words in the box to complete the drawing.

| adenine | cytosine | guanine | thymine |

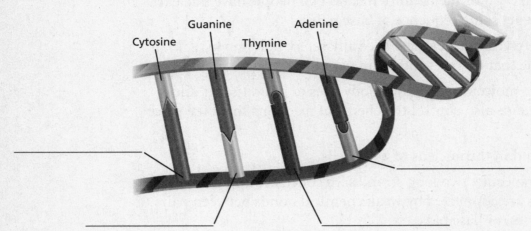

Making a DNA Profile (pages 90–91)

Key Concept: To make a profile, scientists must collect, isolate, multiply, and sort DNA.

▶ Some sections of DNA are non-coding, meaning they do not contain instructions for making a protein. In non-coding DNA, a sequence of bases can be repeated many times. The number of times a sequence repeats is an inherited trait.

▶ A **DNA profile** is a distinctive pattern of DNA fragments. The pattern is used to match a biological sample to an individual.

▶ After a sample containing DNA is collected, the DNA must be isolated, or removed, from the sample.

▶ **Replication** is the process by which a DNA molecule makes a copy of itself. A forensic scientist can use this process to increase the amount of DNA for testing. Only selected segments of non-coding DNA are copied.

▶ The fragments of DNA left after "multiplication" can be sorted to produce a visual profile.

Use your textbook and the ideas on page 90 to answer these questions.

4. What must a CSI be careful to avoid while collecting DNA?

_____

5. What happens when a scientist spins blood at high speed? Circle the letter of the correct answer.

   a. The cells separate from the liquid.

   b. DNA is released from white blood cells.

   c. DNA settles out of the mixture.

6. The steps of DNA replication are listed below. Place the numerals 1 through 4 on the lines to put the steps in the correct sequence.

   a. Bases bond to bases on the single strands. _____

   b. The strands separate and unwind. _____

   c. Bonds between base pairs break. _____

   d. The original molecule and the copy rewind. _____

Probability (page 92)

Key Concept: As the number of segments tested increases, the probability of two people having the same DNA profile decreases.

▶ It is possible that two people will have the same DNA profile, but it is not probable. **Probability** is a measure of the chance that an event will happen.

▶ Scientists can calculate the probability of two people having the same number of repeats in a given DNA segment.

▶ Scientists often test at least 13 different segments.

Use your textbook and the ideas above to answer these questions.

7. What is the probability of a tossed coin landing heads up?

_____

8. Why do courts accept DNA evidence? Circle the letter of the correct answer.

   a. No two people have DNA with the same sequence of bases.

   b. The probability of two people having the same DNA is very low.

   c. A DNA profile is based on sequences of non-coding DNA.

Uses of DNA Profiles (pages 93–95)

Key Concept: DNA profiles are used to connect a suspect to a crime. They also help solve cold cases, free the innocent, identify human remains, and protect endangered species.

▶ If police have a suspect, the lab can compare a profile of the suspect's DNA to one prepared from evidence at the crime scene. Police can also search for a suspect in a database of DNA profiles.

▶ DNA testing may be used to solve **cold cases**—old, unsolved cases. DNA testing may also be used to prove that a prisoner's claim of innocence is true.

▶ To identify human remains, scientists can use DNA that is found outside the nucleus.

▶ DNA testing can help protect endangered species. An **endangered species** is a species whose numbers are so small that it is at risk for disappearing from the world.

Use your textbook and the ideas above to answer these questions.

9. Blood from a man was used to make DNA profile 1. Use the graph on the right to draw DNA profile 2 for the man's identical twin.

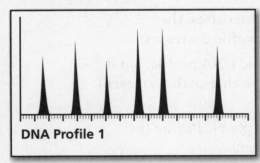

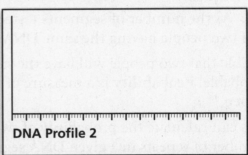

10. Circle the letter of any item that can be found in CODIS.

   a. DNA profiles prepared from crime scene evidence

   b. DNA profiles of known offenders

   c. DNA profiles of missing persons

11. Is the following statement true or false? Scientists need biological evidence in order to use DNA testing to solve a cold case. _____

12. How does DNA that is found outside the nucleus differ from nuclear DNA? Circle the letter of the correct answer.

   a. It is more likely to decay.

   b. It comes only from a person's mother.

   c. It is not found in every cell.

Lesson 3-4 Reading and Note Taking Guide

Handwriting and Voice Identification (pages 96–99)

Handwriting Identification (pages 97–98)

Key Concept: Handwriting experts look at the style of the handwriting and for content clues.

▶ People have distinctive handwriting styles.

▶ Handwriting experts look at whether the letters in a writing sample are separate or joined. They also look at the shape, size, and slant of letters.

▶ It is easier to compare writing samples when the samples contain some of the same words.

▶ Some of the content clues that experts look for in writing samples are word choice, spelling, and punctuation.

▶ Sometimes an expert has to determine whether a document, such as a check, has been altered.

Use your textbook and the ideas above to answer these questions.

1. Circle the letters of all the choices that describe features that hand-writing experts look for in a sample.

   a. size and shape of letters

   b. whether the sample is easy to read

   c. whether letters are joined together or separate

2. Circle the label of the writing sample that best matches the evidence from the crime scene.

   Evidence

   Meet me in the park at midnight.

   Sample 1

   Bob owes me twenty dollars.

   Sample 2

   Remember to feed the cat.

   Sample 3

   *Ice cream
   Paper towels
   Orange juice
   Salad dressing*

3. What can an examiner do if he suspects that the writing on a document has been erased?

_____

_____

Voice Identification (pages 98–99)

Key Concept: To compare voice samples, analysts can graph the sound or listen to the recordings.

▶ A sound spectrograph changes sound waves into electrical impulses. These impulses can be graphed and viewed on a computer screen. The graph, or **voiceprint,** plots the pitch and loudness of sound over time.

▶ Some features of a person's voice will show up in a voiceprint. Some can be recognized by a person listening to a recording.

Use your textbook and the ideas above to answer these questions.

4. A person called a second person and left a threatening voice mail. Investigators have a possible suspect. What would an analyst need in order to determine whether the suspect left the message?

_____

_____

5. Complete the following sentences. A voice analyst is comparing two recordings or graphs. If he finds 20 or more points in common, he can _____ a suspect. If he finds 20 or more differences, he can _____ a suspect.

Lesson 3-4 Skills Lab
Measuring Writing

Problem

What measurements can you use to describe a
writing sample?

Background

Sometimes investigators use a handwriting expert to help
solve crimes. The expert's job is to decide if the same person
wrote two handwriting samples. Experts use both handwriting style and content to analyze samples. One method
they use to analyze style is to measure the slant of letters and
the spaces between letters. In this activity, you will use this
method to analyze your own handwriting.

Skills Focus

measuring, calculating, designing experiments

Materials

• ruled paper
• metric ruler
• protractor
• tracing paper

Procedure

1. Write the following words on a sheet of ruled paper: Forensic scientists analyze evidence. They do not convict or clear suspects.

2. Draw a line through each letter in the sample as shown in the photo on page 100 of your textbook. The line should have the same slant as the letter.

3. Select a line. Use a protractor to measure the angle the line makes with the ruled line on the paper. Measure the angle for two other lines. Enter your data in the data table.

4. Place tracing paper over your sample. Draw vertical lines between each letter. Select a pair of lines. Use a metric ruler to measure the distance between the lines (the spacing) in millimeters. Repeat the measurement for two other pairs of lines. Record your data.

Data Table				
Feature	Trial 1	Trial 2	Trial 3	Average
Slant (degrees)				
Spacing (mm)				

Analyze and Conclude

1. **Designing Experiments** Why do you think you were asked to make three separate measurements for slant and spacing?

   _____

   _____

   _____

2. **Calculating** Calculate the mean, or average, slant and spacing. Enter the results in the data table and record them on your sample.

   _____

   _____

3. **Designing Experiments** Select another feature of the writing sample that you could measure. Describe the method you would use to measure this feature.

   _____

   _____

   _____

4. **Interpreting Data** Make a class display of the samples. What is the range of data for average slant? For average spacing?

   _____

   _____

5. **Drawing Conclusions** How could measurements be used to identify a writing sample?

   _____

   _____

   _____

   _____

Communicating

Pick two samples to compare. Write a paragraph explaining how an analyst could tell that the samples were written by different people.

_____

_____

_____

_____

_____

_____

_____

_____

Lesson 3-1) Laboratory Investigation 8

Latent Clues

Problem

How are fingerprints collected and used to identify a suspect?

Background

Several music CDs are missing. The thief took the CDs but left the plastic cases. The cases have fingerprint evidence. It is your job to dust the cases for fingerprints. Then you must lift the prints and analyze them to find the thief.

Skills Focus

observing, classifying, interpreting data

Materials

Part 1
- newspaper
- CD case
- magnetic fingerprint wand
- magnetic fingerprint powder
- fingerprint-lifting tape
- fingerprint-lifting cards

Part 2
- hand lens
- 6 sets of fingerprints from suspects
- lifted fingerprints from Part 1

Safety First 🦠 🧥 🖐 🥽 🧼

Wear goggles, a lab apron, and plastic gloves. Do not inhale the fingerprint powder. Clean up any powder spills. Spilled powder will make the floor slippery. Wash your hands with warm water and soap after the activity.

Procedure

Part 1: Lifting Fingerprints

In this part of the activity, you will dust the CD cases for fingerprints and lift three prints.

1. Put on goggles, a lab apron, and plastic gloves. Spread newspaper over your workspace. Locate the CD case that your team will analyze. Handle the CD case only by the edges to avoid damaging the fingerprint evidence.

2. Push the plunger of the magnetic fingerprint wand all the way down. Dip the tip of the wand into the container of magnetic fingerprint powder. Pull the wand up out of the powder and gently shake the wand over the container to remove any extra powder.

3. Brush the powder over the CD surface using light strokes in several different directions. Do not touch the surface of the case with the wand because touching the case may damage the prints.

4. When you are finished dusting for prints, hold the wand over the container and lift the plunger. Allow any remaining powder to fall into the container. Gently tap the side of the CD case on the newspaper to remove any extra powder. Push the plunger forward again and use the wand to pick up the extra powder from the newspaper. Return the extra powder to the container.

5. Examine the dusted prints and choose the one that looks like the clearest and most complete print. Peel off the backing from a piece of fingerprint-lifting tape. Place the edge of the tape just beyond the edge of the print. Slowly roll the tape over the print. Press down hard enough to stick the print to the tape. Do not press too hard or you will damage the print.

6. Lift the tape from the surface in one slow, even motion. Immediately place the tape on the shiny side of a fingerprint-lifting card. Turn the card over and fill in as much of the requested information as possible.

7. Select the next best fingerprint and repeat Steps 5 and 6. Use the same process to lift a third print. When you are finished, you should have an unidentified fingerprint on each of three cards.

Part 2: Comparing Fingerprints

In this part of the activity, you will classify the print you lifted and find ridge details in the print. Then you will find the closest match from the fingerprints taken from suspects.

8. Examine the three unknown fingerprints you lifted from the CD case. Select the print that is the most nearly complete. Set the other two prints aside.

9. Use the hand lens to examine the selected fingerprint. Classify the fingerprint as having a loop, arch, or whorl pattern. Write the pattern name below the fingerprint.

10. Use the hand lens to examine the six sets of fingerprints taken from suspects. Write the pattern name below each print.

11. Use the hand lens again to examine the unknown print. Locate details such as ridge ends, forks, dots, and enclosures. Circle each detail and label it. Refer to Figure 1 on page 75 in your textbook.

12. Examine the page that contains prints from the suspects. Circle all prints that have the same pattern as the unknown print.

13. Use the hand lens to compare the unknown print with each circled print. Look at the fine details in each print. When you find the circled print that most closely matches the unknown print, write the suspect's name under the unknown print. Also write down which finger was used to make the matching print.

14. Follow your teacher's instructions for disposal of extra fingerprint powder. All other materials may be thrown away in the trash.

Analyze and Conclude

1. Were the fingerprints on the CD cases visible, plastic, or latent? Explain your answer.

   _____

   _____

   _____

2. How did the magnetic powder reveal the fingerprints on the CD case?

   _____

   _____

   _____

3. What was your biggest problem when you dusted for fingerprints? How did you solve this problem?

   _____

   _____

   _____

   _____

4. What was your biggest problem when you lifted the prints? How did you solve this problem?

   _____

   _____

   _____

   _____

5. What was the most common detail you found in the unknown fingerprint? How many of these details did you identify?

   _____

6. Based on the fingerprint data that you gathered and analyzed, what can you conclude about the suspects? Explain.

_____

_____

_____

_____

_____

Communicating

Write a brief summary of the process you used to dust, lift, and analyze the unknown fingerprints. In your report, be sure to include the conclusion you reached.

_____

_____

_____

_____

_____

_____

_____

_____

Lesson 3-2 Laboratory Investigation 9

Every Drop Tells a Story

Problem

What conclusions can you draw from bloodstains?

Background

Bloodstains can differ in many ways. There can be a single drop or a large pool of blood. The number and location of drops are important. So are the size and shape of the blood-stains. Analysis of bloodstains can provide clues about what happened during the crime.

   In this activity, you will use different methods to make bloodstains. Then you will analyze and compare them to determine how the stains are different.

Skills Focus

observing, inferring, making models, drawing conclusions

Materials

- newspaper
- fake blood
- meter sticks
- index cards, 5" × 8"
- metric ruler
- copy paper, 8 1/2" × 11"
- graduated cylinder, 10-mL

- masking tape
- plastic syringe, 5-mL
- small beaker or cup
- clipboard
- protractor
- blocks of wood
- string

Safety First 🔲 🔲 🔲 🔲 🔲

Wear goggles, a lab apron, and plastic gloves. Exercise care when you walk on the newspapers, as they may slide out from under your feet. Clean up spills immediately. Wash your hands with warm water and soap after completing the activity.

Procedure

Each team will make a different type of bloodstain. Then, you will measure and analyze the bloodstains made by all the teams. Finally, you will use this information to write a story about how the bloodstains might have been produced.

Part A: Single Drop Bloodstains

1. Put on goggles, plastic gloves, and a lab apron. Spread newspaper over the floor where you will be working. Label an index card *Part A: 15 cm.*

2. Place the labeled index card in the center of the newspapers. Hold a dropper bottle of fake blood upside down over the index card. Use the meter stick to measure 15 cm from the tip of the bottle to the index card.

3. Squeeze the bottle gently until one drop is released and lands on the index card. Remove the index card and set it aside to dry.

4. Label a new index card *Part A: 30 cm* and place the labeled card on top of the newspapers. This time, hold the bottle of fake blood so the tip is 30 cm from the index card. Squeeze the bottle gently until one drop is released and lands on the index card. Set the card aside to dry.

5. Repeat Step 4 for heights of 45 cm, 60 cm, 75 cm, 90 cm, 105 cm, 120 cm, 135 cm, and 150 cm. Remember to label each index card with *Part A:* and the appropriate distance.

6. Arrange the cards in order by distance and allow the blood drops to dry.

Name_____ Class _____ Date _____

Part B: Low- and High-Volume Bloodstains

7. Put on goggles, a lab apron, and plastic gloves. Spread several layers of newspaper on the floor where you will be working. Label a sheet of copy paper *Part B: Low Volume, Multiple Small Drops.* Place the paper in the center of the newspapers.

8. Hold a dropper bottle of fake blood upside down with the tip of the bottle 30 cm above the paper. Gently squeeze the bottle until one drop falls onto the paper.

9. Without moving the bottle, squeeze a second drop so it falls on top of the first drop.

10. From exactly the same height and position, squeeze a third and fourth drop from the bottle. Carefully set the paper aside to dry.

11. Place a new sheet of copy paper on the newspapers. Label this paper *Part B: High Volume, Single Large Drop.*

12. Squeeze the bottle of fake blood to release 2 mL of fake blood into the graduated cylinder. Position the cylinder 30 cm above the paper. Pour the entire volume of blood all at once onto the paper. Leave the paper to dry.

Part C: Bloodstains From a Moving Person

13. Put on goggles, a lab apron, and plastic gloves. Place 12 sheets of copy paper in a row end to end and tape them together. Turn the row of paper over so the paper is tape-side down. Spread newspaper underneath and on both sides of the copy paper. Write *Start* at the end nearest you.

14. Hold the squeeze bottle of fake blood at about hip level, with the tip pointing down. Hold the bottle away from your body so that you do not squeeze blood on yourself. Squeeze the bottle until single drops begin to fall. Continue squeezing the bottle and walk at a normal pace alongside the row of paper. Let the drops fall onto the paper.

15. Label the papers *Part C: Walking Drops,* and then set them aside to dry.

16. Assemble another set of 12 clean sheets. Write *Start* at the end nearest you. Repeat Steps 14 and 15 but this time very carefully run alongside the paper at a fast pace.

17. Label this set of papers *Part C: Running Drops* and allow them to dry.

Part D: Bloodstains From Arteries

Arteries are major blood vessels. Your goal is to study the force of blood being pushed from an opened artery.

18. Put on goggles, a lab apron, and plastic gloves. Place 30 sheets of copy paper end to end in three side-by-side rows (10 sheets per row). Tape the sheets together. Turn the sheets over, so they are tape-side down. Spread newspaper underneath and around all sides of the copy paper.

19. Squeeze about 6 mL of fake blood into a beaker or cup. Fill a syringe with 2 mL of fake blood. Stand at one end of the three rows of paper, facing the paper. Hold the syringe at waist level. Grasp the barrel of the syringe with your left hand and grip the plunger with your right hand. If you are left-handed, switch the grip.

20. Aim the syringe so that it is parallel to the floor and point the tip toward the rows of paper. Push the plunger forward, applying medium pressure, so that the 2 mL of fake blood spurts out.

21. Fill the syringe with another 2 mL of fake blood. Aim slightly to the left of the first bloodstain and push the plunger again so that an additional 2 mL spurts out.

22. Fill the syringe again and aim slightly to the right of the original stain and push out another spurt.

23. Label this set of papers *Part D: Bloodstains From Arteries.* Allow the papers to dry.

Name_____ Class _____ Date _____

Part E: Angled-Drop Bloodstains

24. Put on goggles, a lab apron, and plastic gloves. Tape the bottom edge of a clipboard to the top of a desk or table. Place newspaper around the clipboard. Label an index card *Part E: 0 Degrees* and clip the labeled card onto the clipboard.

25. Use a meter stick to measure 30 cm above the index card. Position the tip of a bottle of fake blood at the 30-cm mark.

26. Squeeze the bottle gently until one drop of fake blood falls onto the card. Remove the card from the clipboard and set it aside to dry.

27. Label a new index card *Part E: 20 Degrees* and attach the labeled card to the clipboard. Use the protractor to tilt the clipboard so it makes a 20-degree angle with the desktop. Use wooden blocks or books to hold the clipboard in place at that angle.

28. Position the tip of the bottle of fake blood 30 cm above the top portion of the card. Then squeeze gently until one drop of fake blood falls onto the card. Remove the card and set it aside to dry.

29. Repeat Steps 27 and 28 for angles of 40 and 60 degrees. Label each card with *Part E:* and the angle used.

30. Allow the cards to dry.

31. Follow your teacher's directions for disposing of the fake blood.

Analyze and Conclude

1. Locate the index cards from Part A. Measure the width of each bloodstain at its widest diameter. Enter your measurements in Data Table 1. Then, summarize how the diameter of the bloodstains changes as the height from which the blood is dropped is increased.

Data Table 1										
Height (cm)	15	30	45	0	75	90	105	120	135	150
Width (mm)										

_____

_____

_____

2. Locate the sheets from Part B. Examine each bloodstain. In Data Table 2, make a sketch of each stain and describe any differences between the two types of stains.

Data Table 2		
	Sketch	Describe
Low Volume		
High Volume		

Name_____ Class _____ Date _____

3. Locate the sets of sheets from Part C. In each set, select one drop
close to the start, one drop in the middle, and one drop near the end.
In Data Table 3, make a sketch of each selected drop of blood.

Data Table 3		
	Walking	**Running**
Start		
Middle		
End		

4. Near the middle of the Walking Drops sheets, select five consecutive
blood drops. Measure the distance in cm between each pair of drops.
Enter the measurements in Data Table 4. Repeat these measurements
on drops near the middle of the Running Drops sheets and record the
data. Then, find the average distance between drops for both sets.

Data Table 4		
	Walking	**Running**
Drops 1–2		
Drops 2–3		
Drops 3–4		
Drops 4–5		
Average		

5. Locate the set of sheets from Part D. Use one piece of string to produce a straight line thrugh the long axis of each set of stains. Describe what you observe about the three pieces of string.

_____

_____

_____

6. Locate the cards from Part E. Measure the long axis and width of each bloodstain. Measure the short axis at its widest diameter. Enter the data in Data Table 5. Then, summarize how the bloodstains change as the angle is increased.

Data Table 5				
Angle (degrees)	0	20	40	60
Long Axis (mm)				
Short Axis (mm)				

_____

_____

Communicating

Select any two types of bloodstains from this activity and assume that the stains were found at a crime scene. Write a story that could explain what happened at the scene.

_____

_____

_____

_____

_____

_____

_____

_____

Lesson 3-3 — Laboratory Investigation 10

The Power of DNA Evidence

Problem

Can you match the DNA profile from a crime scene sample to a DNA profile of a sample from a suspect?

Background

Electrophoresis (ee lek troh fuh REE sus) is a process used to sort DNA fragments according to their size. An electric field pulls the fragments through a thick gel. Shorter fragments travel farther than longer fragments. Each DNA sample has different DNA fragments. Each fragment concentrates at a different distance from the starting point. The result is a pattern of bands. Each person's DNA produces a unique pattern of bands.

A woman's pet monkey has been stolen. The monkey has been known to bite strangers. A few drops of blood were found on the floor near the monkey's cage. Police have identified two suspects with a long history of stealing valuable monkeys. Your job is to analyze DNA from the blood left at the crime scene and the blood from two suspects. If the DNA matches the DNA of the monkey's owner, then this could be a case of a falsely reported theft. If the DNA from the crime scene matches the DNA of either suspect, then you can tell detectives who should be arrested. Good luck!

Skills Focus

observing, drawing conclusions, communicating

Materials

- gel block with six wells
- electrophoresis chamber
- buffer solution
- 4 DNA samples in microfuge tubes
- 4 micropipettes with metal plungers
- 2 electric cords
- metric ruler, 15-cm
- DNA stain
- staining tray
- beaker, 250-mL
- graduated cylinder, 100-mL
- five 9-volt alkaline batteries
- clock or timer

Safety First! 🧿 🧤 🦺 🔪 ♨ ✋

Wear goggles, gloves, and a lab apron while doing this activity. Clean up all spills. Wash your hands with soap and warm water when you are finished. Handle glass items with care. To avoid electrical shocks, make sure the batteries, cords, and your hands are dry.

Procedure

Part 1: Loading DNA Samples

In this part of the investigation, you will add DNA samples to a gel block. There are six depressions, or wells, at one end of the block. You will add DNA samples to four of these wells.

1. Put on your goggles, an apron, and plastic gloves.

2. Obtain a plastic tray with a gel block. Place the tray in the center of an electrophoresis chamber. The wells should be closest to the black (negative) electrode.

3. Add 200 mL of dilute buffer solution to the chamber. Be sure the surface of the buffer solution is 2–3 mm above the top of the gel. The buffer solution must not touch the electrodes on the side of the chamber.

4. Obtain the microfuge tube labeled Crime Scene DNA. Make sure the sample is at the bottom of the tube before opening the tube. Push the metal plunger all the way to the bottom of a micropipette. Insert the end of the pipette into the tube. Gently pull the plunger up to draw 10 µL (microliters) of liquid into the pipette.

5. Insert the end of the pipette into the first well of the gel block. Be careful not to puncture the bottom of the well with the pipette. Hold the pipette steady and gently press the plunger forward. You should see the dyed sample going into the well as you push the plunger. When the pipette is empty, discard the pipette in the trash.

6. Repeat Steps 4 and 5 for the Suspect 1 DNA, Suspect 2 DNA, and Victim DNA. Use a new pipette each time you load a DNA sample. Be sure to place each sample in a separate well. When you are finished, four wells will contain a sample and two wells will be empty.

7. Make sure the chamber cover is dry and then place it on the electrophoresis chamber.

Part 2: Separating DNA Fragments

In this part of the activity, you will use an electric field to pull the DNA fragments through the gel.

8. Connect five 9-volt batteries as shown in the diagram. Snap the positive terminal of one battery to the negative terminal of another battery. When you are finished, you will have one open negative battery terminal and one open positive terminal.

9. Use the red cord to attach the open positive battery terminal to the red electrode on the chamber. Use the black cord to attach the open negative terminal to the black electrode.

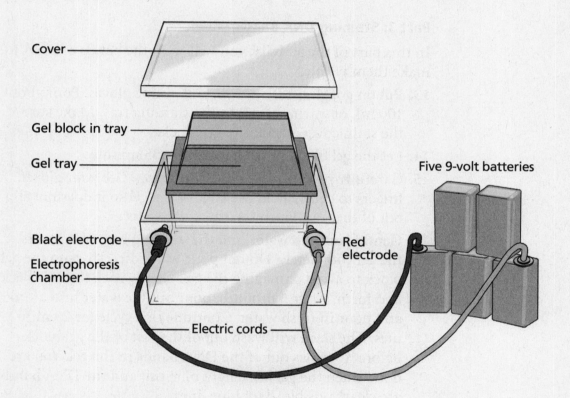

Cover

Gel block in tray

Gel tray

Black electrode

Electrophoresis chamber

Red electrode

Electric cords

Five 9-volt batteries

10. Once the batteries are attached to the chamber, you will see bubbles form along the wires at the bottom of the chamber. If you do not see bubbles, recheck the electric connections.

11. The purple tracking dye will slowly move through the gel toward the end of the chamber with the red (positive) electrode. When the dye reaches the end of the gel block, disconnect the batteries from the chamber.

12. Remove the gel tray from the chamber and use your gloved fingers to push the gel block gently off the casting tray into a staining tray. The gel block is fragile. Use caution not to break the gel block during the transfer.

Part 3: Staining DNA Bands

In this part of the activity, you will stain the bands of DNA to make them visible.

13. Put on goggles, a lab apron, and plastic gloves. Pour about 100 mL of warm stain into the staining tray. Make sure the stain covers the entire gel block.

14. Let the gel block sit in the stain for 35 minutes.

15. Carefully pour off the stain into a sink. Use your gloved fingers to gently hold the edge of the gel so it does not slip out of the tray. Flush the sink with water.

16. Gently pour tap water into the staining tray so it covers the gel completely. Do not pour water directly onto the gel block to avoid damaging the gel. Gently rock the tray back and forth. After 5 minutes, pour out the water into a sink and pour in fresh water. Continue this cycle for 25 minutes. The stain will wash out of the rest of the gel block before it washes out of the DNA bands in the gel. You are done when the gel has a light blue tint and the DNA bands are clearly visible, dark blue lines.

Name_____ Class_____ Date _____

Part 4: Sketching and Measuring DNA Bands

In this part of the activity, you will sketch the bands of DNA and measure how far they traveled in the gel.

17. Leave the gel block in the tray and place the tray on a light-colored surface. Sketch the DNA bands in Data Table 1.

18. For each DNA sample, measure the distance from the edge of its well to the center of each DNA band. Enter the measurements in Data Table 2.

Data Table 1					
DNA From Crime Scene	DNA From Suspect 1	DNA From Suspect 2	DNA From Victim	Empty Well	Empty Well

Data Table 2				
Band	Crime Scene	Suspect 1	Suspect 2	Victim
1				
2				
3				
4				
5				
6				
7				

Analyze and Conclude

1. Why did you have to use a new pipette for each DNA sample?

   _____

   _____

2. What is the relationship between the distance traveled by fragments and fragment length? Where are the shortest fragments of your DNA samples located?

   _____

   _____

   _____

3. Based on the sketches in Data Table 1, which profile most closely matches the profile of the DNA found at the crime scene? Explain.

   _____

   _____

   _____

4. Based on the data in Data Table 2, which profile most closely matches the profile of the DNA found at the crime scene? Explain.

   _____

   _____

   _____

   _____

5. Based on your results, what can you conclude about the person whose DNA matches the DNA found at the crime scene?

   _____

   _____

Communicating

On a separate sheet of paper, write a summary of the results of your DNA analysis. Be sure to state which DNA sample you think matches the Crime Scene DNA. Explain why you reached that conclusion.

Chapter 3 — Chapter Project

Identifying the Thief

Background

In the Chapter 2 Project activity, you narrowed the list of suspects from 36 to 4. In this activity, you will identify the thief. Each remaining suspect should have a different blood type—A, B, AB, and O.

A blood sample was collected from the Missing Masterpiece crime scene. It is your job to use blood typing to analyze this blood. Blood typing involves mixing the unknown blood sample with a liquid, called a serum, that contains either Anti-A or Anti-B antibodies. When you observe the results, you will know the blood type of the blood left at the crime scene. This information will allow you to eliminate three suspects from your list. You will then have one suspect who is most likely the thief.

Skills Focus

observing, inferring, drawing conclusions

Your Goals

Using the directions in this activity and Figure 6 on page 82 of the textbook, you will

- analyze a blood sample from the crime scene to determine its blood type

- determine which of your remaining suspects has the same blood type as the blood found at the crime scene

- follow the safety guidelines in Appendix A

Materials

- blood typing tray
- fake crime scene blood sample
- fake Anti-A serum
- fake Anti-B serum
- toothpick
- clock or stopwatch
- hand lens

Name_____ Class_____ Date _____

Safety First 🫁 👤 🧤 🧯

Wear goggles, a lab apron, and gloves while doing the activity. Clean up all spills immediately. Wash your hands with soap and warm water after the activity.

Procedure

1. Put on goggles, a lab apron, and plastic gloves.

2. The blood typing tray has three depressions, called wells. One well is labeled A and one well is labeled B. Have your teacher place one drop of crime scene blood in each of these wells. (NOTE: You will not use the third well, which is labeled "Rh.")

3. Add a drop of Anti-A serum to Well A. Add a drop of Anti-B serum to well B. Be careful not to touch the tips of the serum bottles to the drops of blood.

4. Use a clean toothpick to mix the blood sample and the Anti-A serum together for 30 seconds. Be careful not to splatter the mixture beyond its well. Throw away the used toothpick in the trash.

5. Using a new toothpick, repeat Step 4 with Anti-B serum and the blood sample in Well B.

6. Carefully place the tray on top of a sheet of white paper with text printed on it. Look through the mixture in each well and try to read the letters on the paper. If you can clearly see the letters, there is no clumping. If you cannot see the letters, or if the letters are not clear, there is clumping. If you are having trouble determining whether or not there is clumping, use the hand lens to view the mixtures. Record your observations in the data table.

7. Wash the blood typing tray with soap and water and dry it with a paper towel. Be careful not to splash the blood and serum mixtures beyond the sink. Clean up any spills immediately. Throw items other than the blood typing tray in the trash.

Data Table	
Well	Clumping or No Clumping
A	
B	

Analyze and Conclude

1. Why was it important to use a new toothpick each time you mixed blood and serum?

   _____

   _____

   _____

2. Based on your results, what can you conclude about the marker molecules in the crime scene blood?

   _____

   _____

   _____

   _____

3. What is the blood type of the crime scene blood?

   _____

   _____

4. Which of the four remaining suspects from Data Table 2 in the Chapter 2 Project has the same blood type as the crime scene blood?

   _____

   _____

5. Based on the results of your previous chapter project investigations, make a list of the evidence that is connected to your final suspect.

   _____

   _____

   _____

   _____

Communicate

Write a summary of your analysis for detectives who are working on this case. In your summary, explain how you used blood typing to determine the type of blood at the crime scene. Use the information in the table on page 83 of your textbook to explain to detectives why blood type, by itself, cannot be used to identify the suspect.

_____

_____

_____

_____

_____

_____

_____

_____

Chapter 3 Video Viewing Guide

Fingerprint Evidence

1. When a person touches a surface, what is transferred from the person's fingertips to the surface?

   _____

2. Why is it possible to use fingerprints to connect a suspect to a crime scene?

   _____

3. What three patterns of ridges are found in fingerprints?

   _____

4. What clues do experts use to distinguish any two fingerprints?

   _____

   _____

5. What is the traditional method for collecting fingerprints?

   _____

6. A fingerprint expert can use a computer to help identify a print. What does the computer do? What does the expert do?

   _____

   _____

   _____

Clues From Bloodstains

7. Why would police officers want to take a class on bloodstains?

   _____

   _____

8. List two variables investigators use to analyze bloodstains.

   _____

   _____

9. According to the person teaching the class, how should scientific evidence that is gathered at a crime scene be used in a trial?

_____

DNA to the Rescue

10. Describe three characteristics an examiner will observe when looking at a hair under the microscope.

_____

_____

_____

11. What are two ways that DNA evidence can be used?

_____

_____

12. Which evidence is more reliable—hair or DNA? Why?

_____

_____

Voice Stress Analysis

13. What type of data does a voice stress analyzer record?

_____

14. What technology could voice stress analysis replace?

_____

15. In this video, an expert states that voice stress analysis should not be used as evidence in a trial. What reason does he give for this statement?

_____

_____

Chapter 4 Building Science Vocabulary

Prefixes

Many English words are made up of several parts. A root is a part of a word that carries the basic meaning. A prefix is a part that is added in front of a root to change the meaning in some way. The word *prefix* is an example. The root *fix* means "to attach." The prefix *pre-* means "before." So a prefix is attached before a root.

You can use the information in the table to help you learn and recall the meanings of some Key Terms in Chapter 4.

Prefix	Meaning	Example
mis-	wrong or bad	**misplace** to put in the wrong place
pro-	moving forward or ahead of	**projection** something that juts out
fore-	before in time, place, order, or rank	**foreman** a man in charge of a group of workers in a factory
ex-	out	**expand** to spread out

Apply It!

Use the information above to answer these questions.

1. The word *internal* means "inside." What does the word *external* mean? _____

2. The word *demeanor* means "behavior." What does the word *misdemeanor* mean? _____

3. When a jury meets to discuss the evidence in a trial, one person is in charge. What do you think this person is called? _____

Name_____ Class_____ Date _____

Building Science Vocabulary (continued)

Latin Word Origins

Many English words come from Latin words. This is true for many words used in court. For example, evidence comes from the Latin word *evidentia*, meaning "clear" or "obvious." The table below lists some Latin origins for legal terms.

Latin Origin	Meaning	English Word
defendere	to ward off or keep away	**defend** *v.* to keep from harm or danger
jus	right or law	**just** *adj.* fair or impartial
populus *publicus*	the people	**public** *adj.* for the benefit or use of all
probare	to test or prove	**probation officer** *n.* a person who supervises people who remain in the community after being found guilty of a crime

Apply It!

Use the information above to answer these questions.

1. A person who is accused of a crime is called a defendant. What do you think a public defender does?

   _____

   _____

2. A jury decides whether a defendant is guilty. The words *jury* and *just* share the same Latin origin. What kind of decision must a jury make?

   _____

3. What do you think people who are supervised by a probation office need to prove?

   _____

   _____

Lesson 4-1 Reading and Note Taking Guide

From Arrest to Trial (pages 106–112)

The Bill of Rights (pages 107–108)

Key Concept: Four of the amendments in the Bill of Rights protect a person's rights before, during, and after an arrest.

▶ The first ten amendments to the U.S. Constitution are known as the **Bill of Rights.** The amendments list the rights that the government promises to protect.

▶ The Fourth Amendment protects people against "unreasonable searches and seizures."

▶ The Fifth Amendment states that people have the right to remain silent when they are asked questions about a crime.

▶ The Sixth Amendment states that a person has a right to a jury trial. A **jury** is a group of ordinary citizens who listen to the evidence at a trial. The jury decides whether the person is guilty. The amendment also protects a person's right to be represented by a lawyer.

▶ The Eighth Amendment states that bail must be reasonable and the punishment set for a crime must not be "cruel and unusual." **Bail** is money or property that is pledged to the court to ensure that a person will appear at trial.

Use your textbook and the ideas above to answer these questions.

1. Choose a word from the box to complete each sentence below.

amendment	right	constitution

a. A _____ describes how a government is organized and what it can do.

b. A _____ is a freedom that all people have.

2. Draw a line from each amendment in Column 1 to a right in
   Column 2 that the amendment protects.

Amendment	Role
Fourth Amendment	**a.** right to a speedy and public trial
Fifth Amendment	**b.** right to remain silent
Sixth Amendment	**c.** protection from unreasonable searches
Eighth Amendment	**d.** protection from cruel or unusual punishment

3. Are the following statements true or false?

   a. A person who is found not guilty of a crime can be tried again for

   the same crime. _____

   b. The government will appoint and pay for a lawyer if a person
   who is accused of a crime cannot afford to hire a lawyer.

   _____

Types of Crimes (page 109)

Key Concept: Crimes are classified as felonies or misdemeanors.

► Laws are rules that everyone in society is supposed to follow. Some
  laws define what acts are considered crimes, and how those crimes
  should be punished.

► A **felony** is a serious crime, such as murder or kidnapping. A
  crime that is less serious than a felony is called a **misdemeanor**
  (mis duh MEEN ur).

Use your textbook and the ideas above to answer these questions.

4. Circle the letter of any crime that is classified as a misdemeanor.

   a. shoplifting

   b. kidnapping

   c. spray-painting graffiti

5. Circle the letter of a right that a felon may lose.

   a. the right to vote

   b. the right to speak freely

   c. the right to a lawyer

6. Is the following statement true or false? A person can be sent to jail

   for a misdemeanor. _____

Making an Arrest (page 110)

Key Concept: Police need probable cause to make an arrest. The person who is arrested is taken into custody and booked.

▶ **Probable cause** is the reasonable belief that a person has committed a crime.

▶ The process that takes place when a person is arrested and taken to a police station is called a booking.

Use your textbook and the ideas above to answer these questions.

7. A police officer sees a person running away from a crime scene. Is the following statement true or false? The officer must have a warrant before she can arrest the suspect.

_____

8. When must investigators read the Miranda warning to a suspect? Circle the letter of the correct choice.

a. as soon as the suspect is arrested

b. before the suspect is booked

c. before the suspect is questioned

Pretrial Procedures (pages 111–112)

Key Concept: At a pretrial hearing, the defendant is charged. The judge may set bail, assign a lawyer, and review evidence. Before a trial, lawyers may reach a plea bargain.

▶ A person who is accused of a crime is called a **defendant**. A defendant will appear before a judge one or more times before trial. A **judge** is the person who controls what takes place in a courtroom.

▶ The lawyer who represents the state in a criminal case is the **prosecutor**. The prosecutor decides what crime a defendant will be charged with.

▶ One decision made at a pretrial hearing is whether a defendant will be released without bail, released with bail, or held until trial.

▶ If a defendant cannot afford a lawyer, the judge can assign a lawyer. This lawyer may be a **public defender**, a lawyer who works for the state.

▶ At a pretrial hearing, a judge may be asked to dismiss a case for lack of evidence or to exclude certain evidence from trial.

▶ Most criminal cases do not go to trial. Instead, they are resolved by a **plea bargain**, an agreement between the prosecutor and the defense.

Name_____ Class_____ Date _____

Use your textbook and the ideas on page 129 to answer these questions.

9. Choose a word or phrase from the box to complete the following sentences.

prosecutor	public defender	judge

   a. A _____ represents a defendant who cannot afford to hire a lawyer.

   b. The _____ is the lawyer who represents the state in a criminal case.

   c. If a defendant does not have a lawyer, a _____ can assign one.

10. Why are criminal cases brought in the name of the state?

   _____

11. In which of these situations would a judge be likely to deny bail? Circle the letter of the correct choice

   a. The defendant cannot afford a lawyer.

   b. The defendant has no ties to the community.

   c. The defendant is charged with a misdemeanor.

12. What is one reason a judge might decide to exclude, or keep out, evidence from a trial?

   _____

13. A defendant agrees to plead guilty. What can the prosecutor do in return? Circle the letter of each statement that is true.

   a. The prosecutor can reduce a charge to a less serious crime.

   b. The prosecutor can agree to a lighter punishment.

   c. The prosecutor can dismiss some charges.

14. What is an advantage of plea bargains?

   _____

15. List two reasons why plea bargains are controversial.

   _____

   _____

   _____

Name_____ Class_____ Date_____

Lesson 4-2 Reading and Note Taking Guide

Presenting Evidence in a Trial (pages 113–120)

In the Courtroom (page 114)

Key Concept: In a courtroom, each person has a role and an assigned place. The judge makes sure that everyone behaves and follows the law.

▶ The judge controls what happens in a courtroom. A law enforcement officer called a **bailiff** helps the judge keep order in the court.

▶ A court reporter makes a record of everything that the lawyers, judge, and witnesses say.

▶ The court clerk keeps the schedule of cases and makes notes summarizing what happens in each case.

Use your textbook and the ideas above to answer these questions.

1. Each person has an assigned place in a courtroom. Add the missing labels to the drawing below.

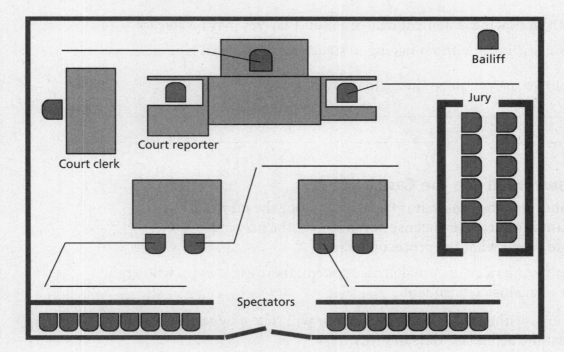

2. When lawyers disagree, who uses the law to decide who is right?

_____

3. Who is responsible for swearing in witnesses?

_____

A Jury Is Chosen (page 115)

Key Concept: An impartial jury makes its decision based only on the facts presented in court.

▶ One duty of United States citizens is to serve on a jury.

▶ In most criminal trials, there are 12 jurors.

▶ Potential jurors are often asked questions by a judge or by opposing lawyers. This process is designed to eliminate jurors who might not make a fair decision.

▶ Before the trial begins, the judge gives instructions to the jury.

Use your textbook and the ideas above to answer these questions.

4. There are rules about who can serve on a jury. Circle the letter of each statement that is true about jurors.

   a. They must be United States citizens.

   b. They must be age 18 or older.

   c. They must live in the district where the trial is held.

5. Is the following statement true or false? A lawyer may be able to dismiss a juror without having to state a reason. _____

6. List two instructions a judge may give a jury.

   _____

   _____

The Lawyers Argue the Case (page 116)

Key Concept: The prosecutor tries to convince the jury that the defendant is guilty. The defense needs to give the jury at least one reason to doubt what the prosecutor says.

▶ In the American criminal justice system, there are lawyers who argue for or against a defendant.

▶ In an opening statement, a prosecutor will state a hypothesis about what the defendant did, and why.

▶ In an opening statement, the lawyer for the defense may point out places where the prosecutor's case is weak.

▶ After the witnesses have spoken, the lawyers make closing statements in which they review the evidence.

Use your textbook and the ideas on page 132 to answer these questions.

7. Why are prosecutors like scientists? Circle the letter of each statement that is true.

   a. They collect evidence.

   b. They test evidence.

   c. They develop hypotheses.

8. Use the words in the box to complete the following sentences.

review	preview

   a. During an opening statement, a prosecutor may

      _____ the evidence.

   b. During a closing statement, a prosecutor may

      _____ the evidence.

Visual Evidence (page 117)

Key Concept: Lawyers use exhibits to present a crime scene, connect a defendant to a crime, or explain scientific evidence.

▶ An **exhibit** (eg ZIB it) is a physical object that is used to make a point in court.

▶ Forensic scientists may use diagrams and charts to explain scientific evidence.

Use your textbook and the ideas above to answer these questions.

9. Draw a line from each goal in Column 1 to an exhibit in Column 2 that might be used to achieve that goal.

Goal	**Exhibit**
present a crime scene	a. enlarged long-range photos
connect a defendant to a crime	b. model of DNA
explain scientific evidence	c. a cast of a tire impression

10. Circle the letter of each statement that is true.

    a. The court clerk keeps a list of exhibits.

    b. Jurors often take a field trip to a crime scene.

    c. Jurors may watch a video of a defendant being questioned by police.

Oral Evidence (pages 118–120)

Key Concept: Both eyewitnesses and expert witnesses can provide oral evidence in a trial.

► The oral evidence provided by witnesses is called **testimony**.

► The lawyer who calls a witness does a direct examination. During a direct examination, a lawyer cannot ask a leading question.

► An opposing lawyer may object to a question being asked. The judge will sustain or overrule the objection.

► The process in which one lawyer asks questions of another lawyer's witness is called **cross-examination**.

► The defendant has the right not to testify during the trial.

► An **expert witness** is a person who has knowledge of a specific area of study.

Use your textbook and the ideas above to answer these questions.

11. What are witnesses asked to do before they testify?

_____

12. Which of the following statements is the best description of a leading question? Circle the letter of the correct choice.

  a. The answer the lawyer wants is included in the question.

  b. The witness knows the answer to the question.

  c. The lawyer does not know what answer the witness will give.

13. Read the following statements about a cross-examination. Circle the letter of each statement that is true.

  a. The lawyer can ask a witness questions about anything.

  b. The lawyer can ask the witness leading questions.

  c. The lawyer wants the jury to doubt the witness's testimony.

14. Is the following statement true or false? When a defendant does not testify in a trial, the jury can infer that the defendant is guilty.

_____

15. What is different about the testimony of expert witnesses as compared to the testimony of other witnesses?

_____

Lesson 4-3 Reading and Note Taking Guide

The Final Stages of a Trial (pages 124–128)

The Case Goes to the Jury (pages 125–126)

Key Concept: The jurors must meet and discuss the evidence before they decide a case.

▶ The decision that a jury reaches, the **verdict**, must be based on the evidence that was presented.

▶ When the jurors meet, one juror is chosen to manage the discussion. This person is called the **foreperson**.

▶ After jurors review the evidence, they will vote. The verdict must be **unanimous** (yoo NAN uh mus); that is, all 12 jurors must agree.

▶ A jury that cannot agree on a verdict is called a hung jury.

Use your textbook and the ideas above to answer these questions.

1. What does a judge do before a jury meets to discuss a case? Circle the letter of each statement that is true.

   a. The judge reviews the charges.

   b. The judge tells the jury to follow the law.

   c. The judge asks the jury to find the defendant guilty.

2. List three things that the foreperson of a jury does.

   _____

   _____

   _____

3. Complete the graphic organizer about the possible effects of a hung jury.

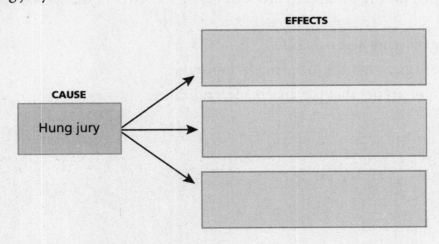

Sentences and Appeals (pages 127–128)

Key Concept: When a defendant is found guilty, the judge must decide on a punishment, or sentence. The defense must decide whether to appeal the verdict.

▶ If a defendant is found guilty of a misdemeanor, the judge may announce a sentence right away. If the crime is a felony, there will be a sentencing hearing, at which supporters of the victim and of the defendant can speak.

▶ For some crimes, the judge may have no choice on the sentence. For other crimes, the judge may have a range of choices.

▶ One possible sentence is probation. A person on **probation** stays in the community and is supervised by a probation officer.

▶ If a defendant is found guilty, the defense can appeal the case to a higher court. An **appeal** is a written request that the verdict in a trial be reversed.

Use your textbook and the ideas above to answer these questions.

4. Is the following statement true or false? If a defendant is found not

   guilty, the prosecutor can retry the case. _____

5. Circle the letter of each factor that can affect the sentence a defendant receives for a crime.

   a. the type of crime

   b. the impact of the crime on a victim

   c. guidelines set by lawmakers

6. Is the following statement true or false? A person who is on proba-

   tion is free to live in any community. _____

7. What can happen during the appeal process? Circle the letter of the correct answer.

   a. The defense presents new evidence.

   b. The defense argues that the judge made a mistake.

   c. The prosecutor argues that the jury made a mistake.

Chapter 4   Skills Lab

Making A Scale Model

Problem

How can you make an accurate scale model of a crime scene?

Background

During a trial, the jury usually does not visit the crime scene. Having an accurate model of the crime scene can help the prosecutor explain to the jury how a crime was committed. In this activity, you will make a scale model of the Missing Masterpiece crime scene.

Skills Focus

making models, measuring, calculating

Materials

- metric ruler
- 2 pieces of graph paper
- 2 pieces of cardboard
- transparent tape

Procedure

Use the measurements in the sketch on page 121 and the illustration on page 1 of your textbook to make a scale model of the Missing Masterpiece crime scene.

1. Count the number of squares on the long edge of your graph paper. Divide the width of the crime scene by the number of squares. The result is the scale of your model. For example, one square might represent 0.20 m.

2. On one piece of graph paper, make a floor plan of the crime scene. The plan should show what you would see if you viewed the crime scene from above. Include the driveway and other objects outside the house.

3. On the second piece of graph paper, make a scale drawing of the wall and doorway.

4. Complete the model by taping each piece of graph paper to a separate piece of cardboard. Then tape the wall to the floor so that the wall is at a right angle to the floor.

Name_____ Class_____ Date _____

Analyze and Conclude

1. **Calculating** What scale did you use for your model? How did you determine this scale?

   _____

   _____

   _____

2. **Making Models** Describe how you used the lines on the graph paper to help you place the objects in your model.

   _____

   _____

   _____

3. **Comparing and Contrasting** How are your scale model and the illustration on page 1 of your textbook different? How are they similar?

   _____

   _____

   _____

   _____

4. **Designing Experiments** Your model is based on an illustration rather than an actual crime scene. How do you think this approach affected the accuracy of your model?

   _____

   _____

   _____

Communicating

Pretend that you are the prosecutor. Explain how you might use your model during the trial of the Missing Masterpiece thief.

_____

_____

_____

_____

_____

Lesson 4-2 Laboratory Investigation 11
Expert Opinions

Problem

How do expert witnesses prepare for a trial?

Background

During this activity, you will assume the role of an expert witness. You will analyze evidence and decide the best way to present the results during a trial. Good expert witnesses provide jurors with the background information they will need to understand the evidence. They also provide specific facts to support their opinions.

Skills Focus

interpreting data, making judgments, communicating

Materials

- test results
- hand lens
- ruler
- protractor

Procedure

Part 1: You Are the Print Examiner

A diamond was stolen from a safe at a jewelry store. The CSI found a fingerprint on the safe that did not belong to any of the store's employees. Detectives identified three known diamond thieves who live nearby. Your job is to examine the fingerprint evidence.

1. Your teacher will give you copies of a fingerprint that was lifted from the safe and fingerprints from the suspects. Compare the fingerprint from the safe with the fingerprints from the suspects.

2. In the space below, record the name of the suspect whose fingerprint most closely matches the fingerprint left at the crime scene. Also briefly describe the process your team used to compare the finger-prints. Include specific details in your summary.

   _____

   _____

   _____

   _____

3. Jurors will need to understand how fingerprints are used to identify a suspect. What background information do you think they would need?

   _____

   _____

   _____

   _____

4. List two questions a defense lawyer might ask to cast doubt on your analysis of the fingerprint evidence.

   _____

   _____

   _____

5. How might you respond to the questions from the defense lawyer?

   _____

   _____

   _____

Part 2: You Are the Handwriting Expert

A thief stole a dog and left a ransom note demanding $10,000 for the dog's safe return. Detectives identified three suspects. Then they obtained handwriting samples from each suspect. Your job is to determine which writing sample is the closest match to the ransom note.

6. Your teacher will give you copies of the ransom note and writing samples from three suspects. Find the sample with handwriting that is the closest match to the writing on the ransom note.

7. In the space below, record the name of the suspect whose handwriting most closely matches the writing on the ransom note. Also briefly describe the process your team used to compare the samples. Include specific details in your summary.

_____

_____

_____

_____

8. Jurors may not think that handwriting can be used to identify a suspect. What could you say to assure them that this method is reliable?

_____

_____

_____

_____

_____

9. List two questions a defense lawyer might ask to cast doubt on the handwriting evidence.

_____

_____

_____

10. How might you respond to the questions from the defense lawyer?

_____

_____

_____

_____

_____

Part 3: You Are the Trace Evidence Expert

A bank robber handed a note asking for money to a teller. The robber left the note behind. Investigators identified four suspects based on eyewitness accounts and other evidence. They used search warrants to obtain a pen from each suspect. Paper chromatography was used to test ink from the pens and from the note.

11. Your teacher will give you sheets with the chromatography test results. Use the results to determine which pen contains ink that most closely matches the ink on the note left at the bank.

12. In the space below, write the name of the suspect who most likely wrote the note. Also briefly describe the process your team used to compare the chromatography results.

_____

_____

_____

_____

13. Jurors will need to understand how chromatography is used to analyze ink. What background information do you think they will need?

_____

_____

_____

_____

14. List two questions a defense lawyer might ask to cast doubt about the chromatography test results.

_____

_____

_____

15. How might you respond to the questions from the defense lawyer?

_____

_____

_____

Analyze and Conclude

1. What is the role of an expert witness?

   _____

   _____

2. Review the inquiry skills described on pages 7–9 of your textbook. Pick one of the three experts in this activity and select three inquiry skills that the expert would use while analyzing the evidence. Include details of how the expert would use each skill.

   _____

   _____

   _____

   _____

   _____

   _____

3. What does a defense lawyer try to do during the cross-examination of an expert witness for the prosecution?

   _____

   _____

   _____

   _____

4. How can an expert witness prepare for cross-examination?

   _____

   _____

   _____

Communicating

Pick one part of the activity and describe what exhibits you would make to help present the evidence to a jury.

_____

_____

_____

_____

_____

_____

_____

Chapter 4) Chapter Project

Conducting a Trial

Background

It is time to bring your suspect from the Missing Masterpiece mystery to trial. In the first part of this activity, you will work with your team to organize and display your evidence. You will also plan the case for the prosecution. The second part of the activity requires you to think like a defense lawyer. Finally, one team will be selected to prosecute their case. Others will be assigned to act as the judge, defense lawyers, the defendant, the court clerk, and witnesses. The rest of the class will act as jurors.

Skills Focus

making models, inferring, drawing conclusions

Your Goals

You will use the directions in this activity to

- prepare visual displays of your evidence
- develop a strategy for presenting your hypothesis about the crime
- participate in a mock trial

Materials

- poster board
- scissors
- markers
- courtroom fact sheets

Procedure

Part 1: Plan the Prosecution's Case

In this part of the activity, you and your team will prepare exhibits and plan how to present your case to the jury. Your goal is to prove your team's hypothesis about the defendant's connection to the crime. To prove your case, you must present the jury with a clear and logical story that is based on facts.

1. Review the test results from the tire print analysis, chromatography, and blood typing activities. Decide what visual exhibits you need to present your case in court. Enter a brief description of your exhibits in Data Table 1.

Data Table 1	
Physical Evidence	**Description of Exhibit**
Tire prints	
Paper chromatography	
Blood type	
Crime scene	

2. Refer to your list in Data Table 1. Gather any visual presentations you made for the Missing Masterpiece mystery in earlier chapter projects. Then construct the exhibits you listed.

3. Decide on your hypothesis for what happened at the crime scene. Write your hypothesis on the lines below.

_____

_____

_____

_____

4. Decide which witnesses you will call during the trial and in what order you will call them. Also decide what facts or expert opinions each witness will present. Enter the information in Data Table 2.

Data Table 2		
Order	**Witness**	**Facts or Expert Opinions**

5. Look over the evidence, your hypothesis, and your list of witnesses. On a separate sheet of paper, prepare a brief opening statement that presents your hypothesis and summarizes the evidence that the jury will see. Opening statements should be no longer than 3–4 minutes.

Part 2: Plan the Defense Case

6. Make a list of questions you will ask each of the prosecution's witnesses during cross-examination. Your questions should be designed to cast doubt on the evidence presented by the witnesses. Record your questions in Data Table 3.

Data Table 3	
Witness	**Questions for Cross-Examination**

Name_____ Class_____ Date _____

7. Decide which witnesses you will call to testify and in what order. Decide whether or not you will have the defendant testify.

_____

_____

_____

8. On a separate sheet of paper, prepare a brief opening statement—no longer than 3–4 minutes. Use the statement to present a different hypothesis or to point out weaknesses in the prosecution's case.

Part 3: The Trial

Your teacher will now assign roles to teams and to individuals.

9. Your teacher will distribute courtroom fact sheets that describe the roles and responsibilities of each person who participates in a trial. Before the trial, use the fact sheets to learn about the role you have been assigned. When the trial begins, use the fact sheets as a guide for what to say and when to say it.

Analyze and Conclude

1. Did the model of the crime scene and other exhibits improve the effectiveness of witnesses? Explain.

_____

_____

_____

2. Explain how your team decided the order of the witnesses for the prosecution.

_____

_____

_____

3. How effective was the prosecution's case? How could the prosecution have presented a stronger case?

_____

_____

_____

_____

Name_____ Class_____ Date _____

4. How effective were the defense lawyers in challenging the evidence presented by the prosecution?

_____
_____
_____
_____

5. Teamwork is essential in forensic science. Describe the jobs that different members of your team did before and during the trial. Was it helpful to work as a team? Explain your answers.

_____
_____
_____
_____
_____

6. In your opinion, did the jury do a good job? Include details about the jury discussion to support your opinion.

_____
_____
_____

Communicate

You write a weekly column about trials for a newspaper. Write a brief summary of the trial that would give your readers a clear idea of what happened during the trial. Offer your opinion on why the jury found the defendant guilty or not guilty.

_____
_____
_____
_____
_____
_____
_____

Chapter 4 Video Viewing Guide

Bill of Rights

1. The U. S. Constitution divides the government into three branches.

   a. Which branch carries out the laws? _____

   b. Which branch makes the laws? _____

   c. Which branch settles disputes? _____

2. Why were several states hesitant to approve the Constitution?

   _____

   _____

3. What name is given to the first ten amendments to the Constitution?

   _____

4. List the freedoms protected by each of the following amendments to the Constitution.

   I: _____

   IV: _____

   VI: _____

Trial by Jury

5. Who can serve on a jury?

   _____

6. Why do attorneys question jurors before a trial?

   _____

7. What is the role of the jury in a trial?

   _____

   _____

8. List three rights of the defendant in a trial.

   _____

   _____

   _____

9. What is the role of the prosecution and the defense in a trial?

_____

_____

10. Who decides on the punishment when the jury finds a defendant guilty?

_____

Virtual Crime Scenes

11. What is the traditional method for diagramming a crime scene?

_____

_____

_____

12. How does a 3-D laser scanner work?

_____

_____

_____

13. What are three advantages of using a laser scanner to take measurements at a crime scene?

_____

_____

_____

_____

14. How would a 3-D laser scan be useful in a trial?

_____

_____